LESSONS IN LEADERSHIT: DETOXING THE WORKPLACE

©2016

Ana Dutra

Hogan Assessment Systems, Inc.

www.hoganassessments.com

First printing 05-16

ISBN 978-0-9975169-0-6

HOGANPRESS

D0188033

To my beautiful daughters Joanna, Isabella, and Alessandra, who constantly teach me unconditional love, and to my husband Jose, the best life partner I could have ever wished for.

Ana Dutra

June 2016

FOREWORD

Throughout my life, I've been blessed by having great relationships with strong women. When I was an adolescent and my father died, my mother stepped up and became the breadwinner and leader at home, at work, in our church, and in our community. I married a wonderfully strong, intelligent, capable woman: I have a remarkably strong, gifted, and compassionate daughter (and two great boys). And, I work for one of the strongest and most competent female business deans in the world. I was thinking about all of these strong women when I recently read neuroscience studies showing that one of the gender differences that exists between men and women has to do with the connective tissue between the two hemispheres of the brain.

Research done at the University of Pennsylvania Medical School involved imaging the brains of nearly 1,000 adolescents. The studies revealed that male brains have more connections within hemispheres. On the other hand, female brains have more connections between hemispheres. The results suggest that male brains may be optimized for motor skills, and female brains may be optimized for combining analytical and intuitive thinking. This fits with my experience of strong women. It is that sort of connection between the analytical and the intuitive that Ana Dutra makes so powerfully in the book that you hold.

I have known and admired Ana for many years. I met Ana more than 15 years ago when we were on a very strategic leadership assignment for Accenture. It was obvious then that she was a realist, a discerning thinker, an impassioned professional, a caring leader, and a trusted colleague. She had an intuitive and analytically connected brain and she used it to make things better. Her later remarkable work--building and leading Korn Ferry--only added to my admiration. Ana has genuinely seen and done it all. When she called me to say that she was writing a book on leadership, I was delighted but cautious. Her vast experience with leadership science and practice is unparalleled, thus her perspective would be valuable. However, with thousands and thousands of leadership titles on the shelves, what could be missing? When she described how she would approach the topic, my enthusiasm grew.

Ana proposed to attack the issue from the perspective of what goes wrong when leaders succumb to vicious patterns and do damage to themselves, their organizations, their people, and their customers. She proposed something more than just another book of tired bromides and well-worn axioms about what makes for a great leader. She wanted to help us gain greater insight into ourselves and be aware of the traps that we can and do fall in when we attempt to lead. It made me think about the wisdom and power of contrast. When we gain clarity about what we will not do or be, it makes choosing the higher good infinitely easier. In a recent discussion about leadership with the dean of my business school, she mentioned that much of what she learned about effective leadership came from watching anti-mentors. I loved the reference and it too struck a chord with me as I considered the recent focus on positive psychology.

One of the seismic shifts in leadership and human development studies that took place over the last two decades occurred when Dr. Martin Seligman, who was then the President of the American Psychological Association, declared that the focus of his term as president would be aimed at the promotion of mental and emotional health rather than more study of mental illness. His passion paralleled the shift among progressive medical doctors from merely studying illness and pathology to health and well-being. Although many misinterpreted his work to be positive thinking, his impact was huge. I consider him to be a certified genius, a prolific writer, and a captivating speaker, who has done a great service to all of us by leading the charge of positive psychology. Whenever a great movement, such as this begins, along with it comes a perversion. The perversion of positive psychology is the belief that the study of negative behaviors has no value. That's plainly wrong.

If all we focus on is our strengths, we risk crippling blindness to our vulnerabilities. An individual or a company might be one of the most innovative engineering powers of all time. The people in such a company might be renowned for their ingenious capability to solve technical problems and to overcome barriers that perplex and confound others. These same people may be grossly vulnerable due to an inability to consider the ethical dimensions of the problems they face. They may be so effective at using their engineering strengths that they become entirely blind to their moral liabilities. For example, such a group might use their technical genius to defeat tests designed to identify the environmental standards to which their machines must operate. If this is more than a hypothetical, and the company is Volkswagen, then building only on their strengths and blindness to their vulnerabilities may cost them hundreds of billions of dollars and jeopardize their very existence. Clearly this is not what Dr. Seligman ever had in mind.

All of us have clay feet. We all have vulnerabilities. As you read Ana's excellent book perhaps you can relate to the Irritable Tyrant, the User and Abuser, or the No Filter. As I read about the latter, I recounted times when I dominated meetings with my incessant questions, comments, and observations. I'm sure the other participants were hoping that I would fit somewhere else. My experience as a business leader, consultant, executive coach, and business school professor has allowed me to see myself and others play out these roles to our detriment and with great cost to others. This is a strong book by a strong leader. It's the kind of book that is needed in the midst of such a volatile and confusing time when we see the prevalence of leadership imposters. This book allows you to become more keenly aware of your vulnerabilities, and you will benefit from Ana's sagacious advice. You will learn how to steer clear of the shoals upon which many a leadership career and the organizations they led lay in wreckage. By doing so you will benefit personally and, as Ana has intended, you will help detoxify the organizations you lead.

Fred Harburg

Executive Director of the Kellogg Executive Leadership Institute (KELI)
Clinical Professor of Executive Education, Kellogg Graduate School of Management

June, 2016

TABLE OF CONTENTS

INTRODUCTION

LESSONS IN LEADERSHIT

Many years ago, as a new mother of my first daughter, I voraciously read all the books I could find on good parenting. Bookstore shelves are packed with resources for parents, and I was determined to learn world-class parenting skills, using all the teachings in those books. The only problem was that the more I read, the less I could relate to the advice. Despite all of my best efforts, I couldn't hold a candle to the world-class mommies described page after page. My baby wouldn't adhere to a disciplined sleeping schedule and she refused to eat the healthy foods that the babies I read about were enjoying. What was I doing wrong? After reading numerous stories of exemplary parents and children, I started wondering if maybe I just wasn't wired to be what society and experts labeled as a great mom. Overwhelmed and exhausted, I felt like everything that wasn't working was most certainly my fault.

It took many years and a lot of self-doubt to realize that my oh-so imperfect world was actually the norm. Most parents behaved similarly to me and, more importantly, their parenting issues were no different than mine. When my older daughter was a teenager, I came across a book titled *Get Out of My Life, but First Could You Drive Me & Cheryl to the Mall* by Anthony Wolf. Instead of emphasizing best practices, the author described in detail all the imperfections, blips and fiascos that occurred in mother-daughter and parent-child relationships. All of the stories were so familiar, it seemed like the author had been hiding in my kitchen and watching my family! I finally understood that the perfect children, families, and mothers I idealized and relentlessly pursued only existed for brief moments, in a few households, and in many books that should be found in the fiction section of bookstores. By using less-than-ideal parenting examples, and providing tips on how to do better next time, that book taught me more than all of the others combined. What's more, I realized I wasn't alone in struggling to be a good parent, which gave me hope and motivation to do better.

In this way, the world of leadership development is no different than the world of parenthood. All of us have the best intentions and want to get it right, but wanting and doing can be two totally different things. No leader wakes up in the morning thinking– *Today I will lose control, provide unclear directions, and drive my team crazy.* Just like no parent wakes up thinking about doing these things to his or her family. And yet, it happens all of the time. In fact, most of us have witnessed or experienced bad leadership behavior, encountering leaders or bosses who were role models of what *not to do* as leaders. However, after reading leadership books and attending training sessions, we have the impression that the world is full of nothing but admirable leaders who instinctively get things right every time. We hear stories where teams are engaged and motivated, on the same page, and work together to produce great results. Case studies paint pictures of what happens when leaders juggle multiple priorities and manage large numbers of people, and everything happens like clockwork. We can understand how these situations turn out so well, but we rarely experience these ideal scenarios in daily life.

After 28 years of management consulting and leading large global organizations, I've seen how difficult it can be for groups of people—new and very seasoned—to simply work together effectively to get something done. Whether leading a team or reporting to a senior leader, we are bound to face situations when people don't see eye-to-eye, conflicts arise, or productivity comes to a standstill. For many managers and executives, this can be a daily reality. These less-than-perfect situations often provide the most teachable moments, but It isn't always easy to determine how to make improvements or carve out the time to reflect on what went wrong. Most leadership resources and references are typically based on best practices rather than worst practices and provide limited insights on how to avoid or address bad leadership behavior.

Thinking back to how my life was changed by that single book that showed how parent-child relationships aren't perfect, I had the idea to write a leadership book that more accurately reflects the real professional world—the world of leader*shit*.

I wrote this book to help new and experienced leaders transition from leadershit to true leadership. Using real case studies (with names changed to protect the innocent and guilty), this book gives examples of the top offenders, such as the Tyrant and the Manipulator. I use these characters to share the worst practices in the workplace and provide advice on how to effectively handle situations when readers are experiencing leadershit behavior.

This book helps readers identify leadershit traits, both in others and in themselves. Whether it's a manager, a direct report, or peer, readers will learn best practices for responding to leadershit behavior, and actionable suggestions for combatting it in an effective way. Each chapter also provides an opportunity for self-assessment so readers can do some personal reflection to discover whether they are exhibiting any leadershit behavior, and if so, how to make steps toward immediate improvement.

My hope is that this book will help people better identify what bad leadership looks like. But more importantly, I want to help readers raise their leadership standards by identifying what kinds of behavior they are willing to accept from their leaders and others, and how to better conduct themselves when they encounter leadershit. Better leadership allows people to develop more engaged and higher-performing teams; it also improves organizational culture, relationships, and quality of life.

CHAPTER ONE

LEADERSHIT IN TODAY'S WORKFORCE

Let's face it. The working world is rough. Deadlines, work-life balance, and performance pressure—it's all difficult. But what typically makes work the most difficult is interpersonal dynamics and the differences in how people behave and conduct themselves. Often referred to as workplace politics, the *people dynamics* side of business is complex and multi-faceted. Professionals find themselves in diverse groups of individuals, each with personal and professional goals. Balancing these goals with shared organizational goals isn't easy. Even when people have the best intentions, it doesn't always translate through their words and actions.

The boss who never shows appreciation.

The peer who always seems like he's hiding something.

The coworker who loves skirting responsibility and throwing others under the bus. Crunch.

All of us have experienced some of these behaviors at some point in our work lives. If any of these characters are part of your day-to-day work experience, you are dealing with leadershit firsthand. Defined as behaviors that negatively affect coworkers, entire teams and the organization, leadershit soaks up our emotional energy. Instead of focusing on being productive, engaged, and innovative, we fixate on how mad we are that Mary did this, how disappointed we are that John said that, and whether the company is going to implode from the inside out and cost everyone their jobs. And we don't just have these

1

thoughts at work—they follow us everywhere. Negative thoughts and anxiety creep into our evenings and weekends, especially on Sunday nights when the whole workweek looms before us. Unlike in our personal lives where we can unfriend those who offend, disrespect, or annoy us, the ability to unfriend our coworkers is much more limited. More often than not, we're stuck with our colleagues and their bad behavior, unless we find another job. This often leaves us wondering what level of behavior is reasonable for us to tolerate, because these people seem to be trying to drive us insane.

On the one hand, some offenses are black and white; having a strong emotional response seems rational. On the other hand, many fall into a gray area; we begin to second guess ourselves and wonder if we are overreacting. Either way if we are not careful, leadershit can bring out the worst in us and turn us into people we don't like to see in the mirror. No job is worth that.

> **Unlike in our personal lives, where we can unfriend those who offend, disrespect, or annoy us, the ability to unfriend our coworkers is much more limited.**

Leadershit: behaviors negatively affecting coworkers, entire teams and the organization.

So, how much is too much to put up with?

After years of working in large corporations, serving on numerous boards, and managing my own consulting firm, I can tell you definitively that people have put up with way too much leadershit in the workplace. No one takes a new job thinking they will suffer through unnecessary drama, unfair situations, inability to make progress, or a hostile environment, but that's what ends up happening to so many talented professionals. Their situation often starts out okay, but gets worse over time. Like the anecdote of the frog in boiling water, it's hard for people to notice when negative conditions escalate gradually.

When the cool water heats up slowly, the frog doesn't jump out—and neither do most people. We get accustomed to our surroundings, and little by little, it's easy to lose an objective perspective of what's acceptable and what's not. As a result, many people end up spending years in horrible working environments.

Fortunately, many organizations are working hard to combat leadershit. Numerous studies show how much better business outcomes are when employees are engaged, teams are cohesive, and the organizational culture is a collaborative and open one. This has caused a shift in the paradigm of the working world; the soft metrics matter, and account for real business results. How employees treat each other matters. How leaders treat employees matters. If companies want to attract and retain top talent and stay competitive in today's market, it is imperative that they uphold higher standards for the way employees are treated. In fact, the workforce is demanding it.

Much has changed since I entered the workforce almost thirty years ago, but one of the most noticeable changes is the clear, courageous and unapologetic expectation for better leadership. Younger generations today don't comply with unjustified rules and expectations, as older generations once did. Instead, they ask sensible questions and challenge leadership—as older generations have taught them to do. Today's workforce knows their job options and choices, and they hold higher standards for their co-workers, managers, and leaders. In the modern workplace more leaders are held accountable for their behavior, which is different from past workplace norms. Technology has played a huge role in this shift because it's so easy to spread information. Good or bad reputations develop quickly and they're hard to shake.

Younger generations have also seen a sudden downturn in the economy and the erosion of long-term job security. They have witnessed firsthand how putting their heads down and being loyal to a company for years may not yield a reward or be enough to provide job security. Younger workers want their jobs to satisfy their current needs; this viewpoint isn't shortsighted, it's smart. Why put up with negative circumstances when you don't even know if the sacrifice will pay off? Better yet, why put up with negative circumstances at all? Which brings up another good point. Today's employees don't just want a job—they want to be fulfilled by their work. That means respecting and enjoying their coworkers, their boss, and the leaders of the company.

Because employees' viewpoints on all of these factors have become more relevant, companies are now focusing on measuring employees' opinions and leaders' reputations. Annual engagement surveys are the norm at most organizations and 360 leadership evaluations are the new standard for assessing and developing managers. At my executive consulting firm, Mandala Global, I've used 360 evaluations to help uncover leaders' strong points and areas for improvement, as well as assess their personalities and work styles. These assessments help boards and senior leaders examine how successful these employees are in their current roles and how successful they are likely to be if promoted into a new role. The evaluations are always interesting because they allow for a comparison in how a person sees herself versus how others perceive her.

I've been involved in conducting 360 evaluations for so many years that I'd started to notice different types of leaders. After reviewing a self-assessment, I developed a picture in my head of what that individual was like, before ever meeting him or soliciting feedback about him from coworkers. And the vast majority of the time, I was spot-on. For example, if a manager was identified as being impatient, having high standards, and having the tendency to speak without thinking things through, I knew that person offended and intimidated colleagues. Sure enough, when I interviewed his coworkers, I heard horror stories about him yelling at reports and instilling fear in them. Or, if I reviewed a self-assessment where the manager displayed low tolerance for ambiguity or the inability to handle complex situations, I knew she was likely to be described by her coworkers as inflexible, and more than likely a control freak.

The more I saw patterns in how people view themselves and discrepancies in how others view them, the more I became intrigued about different characters in the workplace. I realized that leaders behave in various ways that cause them to be labeled as certain types. Even if coworkers weren't able to put their finger on why a leader rubbed them the wrong way, after reading their self-assessment, I could usually pinpoint the issue. The heart of the matter always came back to the same handful of offenses. I took note of this and tested my theory by conducting more 360 assessments, listening to friends vent about their jobs and bosses, and watching the interpersonal dynamics play out in various professional and volunteer organizations. Through this qualitative and quantitative research, I found that **most leadershit comes down to ten distinct types of offenders:**

- ☐ The Irritable Tyrant
- ☐ The User and Abuser
- ☐ The Manipulator
- ☐ The Chameleon
- ☐ The No-Filter
- ☐ The Landgrabber
- ☐ The Unaccountable
- ☐ The Inauthentic
- ☐ The Poor Communicator
- ☐ The Bad First Impressionist

Some of these types of leadershit can be intentional and even malicious, where the offender is quite self-aware and knowledgeable about the impact his behavior has on other people. Other types are accidental and seem benign—either the individual is not aware of his behavior and its consequences or he just can't help himself even after being made aware of his behavior. Although they vary in intensity, all leadershit behaviors are damaging to the workplace in different ways.

Each of the following chapters is dedicated to a leadershit character type. I explain the type of leadershit offense, how it manifests with bosses, peers, and subordinates, how it is detrimental in the workplace, and, more importantly, what you can do to improve working relations with each type of individual. I also highlight true stories of leadershit in action. (The names and identifying details have been changed to protect the victims.)

It's important to be self-aware and recognize when your behavior aligns with a type of leadershit so you can correct yourself and do better.

In each chapter, scales from the Hogan Development Survey (HDS) are used to describe the leadershit type. The HDS assesses performance risks that interfere with a person's ability to effectively develop and lead a team. The HDS reliably identifies behavioral tendencies that could derail a person's career.

So, for each leadershit profile, I have included a table that provides information from the HDS. This table contains the top three behavioral tendencies that are associated with the leadershit profile being described. In addition, it details the behavior you will see in the workplace from a boss who has this leadershit profile.

This book starts out with the bad behavior that is clearly identifiable. With the right information, you know when it's happening. Deeper into the book, leadershit types that are more subjective and typically fall into a gray area in terms of self-awareness and intention are covered. This category of bad behavior certainly exists, but is more open to interpretation as far as whether the offender is aware of it or can do anything about it.

It's important to note that many leaders occasionally exhibit a combination of these behaviors to varying degrees, depending on the context and their circumstances. For example, nobody is manipulative one hundred percent of the time, but when under pressure or feeling stressed, they are more likely to resort to manipulation than deal with issues directly. Others will lose their composure when they find themselves in threatening situations. Such circumstances will often have leaders drawing on their dark sides, using leadershit behaviors that could potentially derail their careers. They don't behave badly all the time, but they do resort to or lean towards unhealthy, destructive behaviors to varying degrees and frequencies.

You may also see glimpses of yourself throughout these pages—after all nobody is perfect. We all display different levels of leadershit tendencies at times in our lives. Just like any personality attribute, bad leadership behavior exists on a spectrum. It's important to be self-aware and recognize when your behavior aligns with a type of leadershit so you can correct yourself and do better. The red flag is raised when people start to be referred to as one of the characters in this book, because they display certain leadershit behaviors most of the time.

We all deserve a pleasant and productive working environment. I hope this book inspires you to be the change you want to see at your organization.

CHAPTER TWO

THE IRRITABLE TYRANT

The Irritable Tyrant provides some of the most obvious examples of leadershit. The Tyrant is disrespectful, obnoxious, arrogant, and offensive to everybody. Tyrants are detrimental for individuals and organizations alike. The thing people remember most about a tyrannical leader is how she makes them *feel*: nervous, insecure, worried, stupid, embarrassed, and even worthless, affecting and sometimes damaging their lives long after a meeting or interaction is over. Tyrants create a staffing nightmare, contributing to high turnover and low job satisfaction, and chipping away at a positive culture until only rubble is left.

What a Tyrant Looks Like

Research shows that personality is a key determinant of people's ability or inability to behave in the workplace. Personality assessments capture aspects of personality that predict behavior. The Hogan Development Survey (HDS) assesses the dark side of personality, identifying toxic and nonproductive behaviors that can and do derail careers. The table that follows identifies the three HDS scales that a Tyrant will typically score high on (7 or greater on a 10-point scale). Blaming others, overreacting, getting upset and pitching a fit are the behaviors most closely associated with high scores for a Tyrant.

Creating a Monster

A healthy and functional professional work environment is no place for a Tyrant, and yet many workplaces are the

The Tyrant's Leadershit Behaviors	
Three Highest *HDS Scores	How the Tyrant will behave in the workplace based on *HDS scores
Excitability	Overreacts, unpredictable, tense under pressure, easily annoyed by others, critical, moody, inconsistent
Imaginative	Different perspectives/ideas, poor influence and persuasion skills, whimsical and eccentric, potentially creative, but sometimes way off mark, preoccupied, unconventional, unaware of how actions affect others
Bold	Feedback resistant, overestimates talents and accomplishments, does not seek out options, demanding and overbearing, blames others, self-promoting, strong sense of entitlement, no sense of team loyalty
Examples	Sydney Pollack, Steve Jobs, Henry VIII

*The Hogan Development Survey (HDS) evaluates the dark side of personality, identifying overused strengths and toxic assets that will derail careers if the behaviors are not kept in check.

breeding grounds for tyrannical behavior. Some of the qualities and attitudes that are rewarded in the workplace, such as confidence and determination, are the same behaviors that enable Tyrants to climb the corporate ladder. However, when these attributes are overused, they can become toxic. For example, overused confidence may turn into arrogance and a lack of self-awareness; overused determination may turn into bullying. The problem becomes worse when Tyrants keep getting a pass on their behaviors through promotions and other rewards, primarily because they produce great business results. The powerful message sent to the organization is that those who deliver results can get away with murder. In fact, many successful executives display results-oriented behaviors combined with tyrannical behaviors. This causes organizational problems in many ways. Just one of the ways is that these leaders often become role models for less-tenured or less-senior employees, thus creating the breeding ground for more tyrants. Even though Tyrant leaders may find some success in the workplace if they can produce desired business results, their behavior alienates others and contributes to creating a fear-bound culture.

I recently worked with a global pharmaceutical company that was in the process of filling a CFO position. An internal candidate, Charles, was vying for the job, but the board members were unsure if he was the best fit. Charles rose through the ranks by being a fixer. For example, if the South American branch wasn't meeting its financial goals, Charles would travel there to figure out the issues and fix them as quickly as possible. This often meant having difficult conversations about performance, firing tenured employees, dissolving teams, and completing other unpleasant duties. The problem was not *what* Charles did but *how* he did it: in an offensive and disrespectful manner, behaving in ways that would be considered unacceptable in most workplaces. Charles took the challenges head-on and he got the financial results the C-Suite and board wanted. More importantly, he excelled at upward management and his superiors thought highly of him.

Charles was promoted and rewarded for his actions and he thought he had the CFO position in the bag. However, the board had one major issue with promoting Charles. It was brought to their attention that employees hated Charles. In fact, some employees explicitly said that if Charles got the top job, they would leave the company. Charles was able to fool key executives about his true nature for a long time, but the deception didn't last. The stories employees told about Charles in 360 assessments painted a picture of someone who was mean down to the core... and seemed to take pride in it. Although Charles had a good track record of getting results, the board was apprehensive of appointing a leader who was universally disliked. Ultimately, the decision was made to go with an external candidate.

Charles was given the news that he wasn't selected for the position and the reason why. He was outraged. He brought up numerous examples demonstrating that the leadership team had rewarded him for his aggressive approach, including specifically telling Charles that his job wasn't to win any popularity contests. He had a valid point. The organization had encouraged and rewarded his tyrannical behavior, and now they were punishing him. As easy as it is to blame Charles for his predicament, the organization is also at fault. They created the monster, not only giving him permission to behave the way he did, but also rewarding him.

What Can We Learn From This Story?

- For Boards, CEOs, and top leaders:
    - o Rewarding tyrannical behavior may work for your organization in the short-term, but it can come back to bite you. Negative culture and high turnover are expensive problems that are difficult to solve.

- For people who identify tyrannical tendencies in themselves:
    - o Even if repercussions aren't immediate, bad behavior will cause doors to close along the way, preventing you from reaching the top rungs of the corporate ladder (or from thriving if you do get there). Your controlling nature won't stay hidden in the long run, and it's in your best interest to try to change. Make sure you try the exercises and tips at the end of this chapter.

- For consummate Tyrants:
    - o Once you are no longer producing top results, you won't have any rapport or positive

relationships to fall back on. People might respect what you have accomplished, but they won't respect how you've done it.

☐ For the victims of Tyrants:

○ Do not hesitate to speak up when you have been treated disrespectfully. All it takes is one courageous individual for others to realize that they do not need to suffer in silence. Of course, if the top leaders shut you out or don't support you, then the type of culture they support becomes clear. After that, it will be your choice whether you want to remain in that type of organization or leave it.

Tyrannical Female Leaders

In another situation, I worked with a global energy company, conducting 360 leadership evaluations, where leaders were evaluated by their peers in one-on-one interviews. I discovered one top leader had four direct reports who were Tyrants. Four! These managers, three men and one woman, were all knee-deep in leadershit and everyone knew it. Many of the behaviors described in the 360 interviews were similar for all four leaders, ranging from throwing fits, to screaming at people, to throwing staplers at the wall. Even though much of the behavior was the same, I was struck by how the same types of comments came up repeatedly for the female leader and differed from the comments made about the males.

For example, she was described as being overly emotional. Many people brought up her personal life, mentioning that she had a new baby, was the sole breadwinner, and that her husband stayed at home with the children. They attributed her tyrannical behavior to emotional instability from having a stay-at-home husband and trying to be a good parent. Our discussions of this woman were akin to reading the *US Weekly* edition of this company's leadershit. The only thing missing was photos of fashion *faux pas*.

However, when we discussed the male leaders, snarky comments weren't part of the conversation. Not a single person attributed their tyrannical behavior (and trust me, there was a lot of it) to emotional or personal problems. No one mentioned the male leaders' lives outside the office or related any of that to their actions at work. In fact, numerous employees described the male Tyrants as having high standards, but being a little rough around the edges.

Most important, when I met with the boss of these four Tyrants to share the feedback, he made similar comments regarding the males and the female leader. It amazed me how quickly the woman's personal life was brought up, exposed, and used as context for her emotional behavior while the men's personal lives were never a consideration in our discussions.

I thought hard about this feedback and put my feminist thoughts in check because I wanted to give everyone the benefit of the doubt. Maybe the male leaders were borderline Tyrants, and maybe Mrs. Crazytrain really was bringing her personal life to the office. I met with the lucky senior leader, who managed these Tyrants and their boss, to share the results of the interviews and to dig deeper about what was really going on. I wasn't surprised to hear that the female leader was on par with the males in terms of tyrannical behavior—all four were intimidating and often insensitive. However, the main difference was how other employees and the Tyrants' direct supervisor reacted to this behavior—they were more accepting of it from men than women.

What Can We Learn From This Story?

Gender equality in our society has come a long way in the past few generations, but women still have a double bind in the workplace. Women walk a fine line of being too passive to be effective leaders and too domineering to be liked. This complicated topic has been addressed by successful female leaders like Sheryl Sandberg in her book *Lean In*. Men and women are viewed through a different lens in the workplace, whether we like to admit it or not. It takes less leadershit behavior for a woman to be seen as a Tyrant than it does for a man. Is this fair? Of course not. Is it a reality? Yes.

☐ Think about Tyrants you have encountered in the workplace. Have you viewed or described their actions differently based on gender? If so, be aware of this and try to remain impartial, making sure you hold male and female leaders to the same standards. The same is true for your peers. How often are people's personal situations brought up as a justification or context for unacceptable behaviors? If you see this happening to some people at work and not others, especially regarding demographics such as sex, race, or age, take responsibility and point it out.

☐ In your organization, how often do men get a pass for tyrannical behavior? How often are women passed up for promotions because of tyrannical behaviors? The best thing you can do in this situation is to speak up and point out the inequality in career advancement opportunities by citing facts and examples, keeping your biases and emotions out of the conversation.

☐ Do you know of anyone in your organization who was promoted despite his or her tyrannical behaviors? If the answer is yes, suggest criteria be added to the promotion process to assess behavior and interpersonal communication. Leadership teams can say they support a collegial, respectful, and collaborative culture, but if they promote people who don't support those cultural values, they are not being honest.

The Perils of a Ruthless Tyrant

Although I wasn't able to give him a 360 evaluation, it's safe to say King Henry VIII was a ruthless Tyrant. He became dangerous when he gained enough power to do whatever he wanted, and people were too afraid to confront him about his horrific behavior. As a result, he beheaded numerous wives and courtiers as his subjects looked on, too scared to speak up or step in. Hopefully your office doesn't have a guillotine, but a lack of medieval execution devices doesn't stop the ruthless Tyrant from wreaking havoc on all who cross his path.

Several years ago, I worked with Lilian, a CEO who was a ruthless Tyrant; I witnessed first-hand the damage she caused to those around her. Lilian had a tendency to lose her temper at the drop of a hat. She blew things out of proportion and looked for people to blame. Sometimes it seemed like she was picking a fight simply because she enjoyed it. People thought her emotional reactions were sometimes out of her control and that she was disturbed. This created deep fear in anyone who shared her company.

The staff was keenly aware of Lilian's leadershit and they did their best to avoid her. When Lilian was in the office, you knew it immediately; the room's vibe transformed and people weren't themselves. It was like a nasty storm had rolled in and people were trying to hunker down and wait it out. Employees shut their doors and hid. If they had to come out, they would peek out to see if Lilian was in view. If so, they would shut the door and wait until she went away. Everyone had an alternate route to the restroom or coffee room just to avoid walking past Lilian's office, because she had a habit of calling people in randomly to yell at them.

One afternoon, I had an unavoidable meeting with Lilian and her Chief Strategy Officer (CSO) to discuss an important project. Lilian started the meeting belittling the CSO for taking a vacation day right before the project started, even though the CSO had requested the day off months in advance. She continued, grilling him with difficult questions that no one could have anticipated or answered. While the CSO was stammering, sweating, and struggling to respond, Lilian asked him why the company was even paying such a stupid person who knew nothing and did nothing. Finally, Lilian excused the CSO from the meeting and told him to go back to his desk.

When Lilian and I were alone in the meeting room, I said, "You should be ashamed of yourself for treating somebody like that."

Lilian burst out laughing. She said, "Wasn't that great? It was so much fun!"

Having worked with Lilian for years, her answer didn't surprise me. Obviously, she was aware of her tyrannical behavior and didn't feel bad about it. In fact, she rather enjoyed it. This is the worse type of Tyrant, because there's little hope for change.

When the meeting was over, I walked back to my office. That's when I saw paramedics go into the CSO's office. He had gone back to his desk and had a stroke. My colleagues and I watched in horror as they carried him away on a stretcher. Fortunately, he survived, but after years of physical therapy, he is still relearning how to talk.

What Can We Learn From This Story?

☐ When you don't hold Tyrants accountable for their behavior, it can escalate to bullying and harassment. Leaders at all levels must be held accountable for their behavior, even CEOs. A system should be put in place for regularly assessing all leaders, and coaching those who aren't successfully managing or working with others. Without checks and balances for leaders at the top, leaders like Lilian are unstoppable, invincible and dangerous.

☐ Ruthless Tyrants cause undue stress in the workplace. If you know this well, you might be a victim of a Tyrant. Not only is stress bad for your personal health, it damages the health of the organization. A tyrannical leader can cause enough stress to send you over the edge or to the hospital.

☐ Even when you know you are in a negative work situation because of a Tyrant boss, you probably think nothing can be done to help the situation. This is not the case. Tyrants will eventually cross the line—not just of what is appropriate, but also what is legally acceptable. As an employee, you should be well aware of your legal rights. In extreme cases, do not hesitate to use your company's confidential employee hotline or meet with Human Resources if a colleague or a boss has clearly crossed the line.

Once a Tyrant, Not Always a Tyrant

Leaders are capable of shedding their tyrannical persona, but it takes self-awareness and the will to change—a combination that many Tyrants, unfortunately, don't have. It's easy to assume that Tyrant leaders know they're Tyrants. Even though that's true for some leaders, others live in a state of ignorance. Instead of acting maliciously to hurt others, they are blind to how their words and actions negatively impact those around them.

Several years ago, a friend of mine was working with Jason, a man who had no idea his tyrannical behavior was out of line. In fact, he didn't even realize his behavior was upsetting others. Jason was a great employee, but a terrible manager. If a senior executive asked him to climb Mount Everest, he would do it with a smile. But if he had to take a team with him, they would be dead before he reached the top and he wouldn't have even noticed. Just like Charles, Jason was passed up for a promotion because of his tyrannical behavior, and giving him more power didn't seem like a smart idea. Unlike Charles' situation, senior leaders never directly encouraged Jason's behavior, but they failed to give him the feedback he needed to change his behavior. As a result, Jason was shocked to learn there was a problem with his behavior.

When the Human Resources leader spoke with him, she let Jason know he could turn things around and within a few years try again for a promotion. Jason didn't want to wait that long. He quit and got a job at another company where he didn't have to dig his way out of a bad reputation.

A few years later, the Human Resources leader heard that Jason had turned things around; he had a new level of awareness and cared enough to become a better leader and a better person. They reconnected and had lunch. He told her he had been going through a lot of health issues when they'd last worked together. He hadn't realized his personal problems were manifesting in work relationships and he felt bad about treating his colleagues poorly.

How to Change

Jason's story gives us hope and shows that change is possible. Whether you work with a Tyrant or notice tyrannical tendencies in yourself, there are numerous strategies and exercises that can contribute to change.

Helping the Tyrant

Self-awareness is the first step to ending a Tyrant's reign. Tyrants must first understand that their behavior is unacceptable in the workplace. Cite specific examples as evidence, rather than relying on vague explanations that are emotionally based. Organizations may want to use an assessment instrument such as a 360 to help them collect objective data that can be shared with the Tyrant.

Some Tyrants have low self-awareness, so be prepared that this conversation may come as a shock to them. On the flipside, others have high awareness of their tyrannical tendencies, but they might not fully grasp how it affects others. In fact, they may view their behavior in a good light because it helps them get things done, but they remain oblivious to the toll it takes on others. In either case, it is essential that Tyrants become aware of and evaluate their behavior.

Willingness to Change

After Tyrants gain an awareness of their behavior, they will be faced with the decision to change. Changing behavior can be a painful process for Tyrants, because they are in their comfort zone when behaving tyrannically. The best way for Tyrants to see the value in changing their behavior is for them to know and to think about the consequences and implications of not changing it. In addition, it can be helpful for Tyrants to know the positive outcomes they could achieve by changing their behavior. This is where motivation plays a major role. When people are extrinsically motivated, the prospect of losing a job or a promotion or making a lower bonus can be powerful motivators to change. When people are intrinsically motivated, self-reflection around what kind of leader they want to be is the most effective trigger of change. Even though both types of motivation can work, intrinsic motivation is much more likely to support lasting change.

The following exercise can help bring out intrinsic motivation to become a better leader:

Imagine and/or visualize that after you retire, a person you care about dearly, such as a child, parent, or friend, bumps into somebody who used to work with you. This colleague doesn't know that the person they are talking to is your loved one. Suddenly your name comes up and your colleague makes a few comments about you. Take a moment and think of what you would want your loved one to hear. Would you like it to be positive? Or negative? Wouldn't it be nice to hear, "I miss John dearly? He was an inspiring, caring and respectful leader. Tough but fair."

How would you feel if the feedback was negative? And instead, your loved one heard something like, "We are so relieved that John retired. We threw a party when he was gone. People hated to work for him. He was obnoxious and a nightmare."

Which John would you like to be? Which comments would you like your children to hear? Remember, you are in control of how people will remember you.

Seeing the Tyrant in Yourself?

Hoping for change isn't usually enough to make it happen; you need to have a plan. A good professional coach or leadership development program that has metrics and goals can make an impact, but the help of a few colleagues can also be powerful. You should give permission to a few trusted colleagues who can give you feedback about your behavior and point out when you start to behave inappropriately. These colleagues can also discuss with you how bad behavior affects professional relationships, business deals, and office morale.

You should also make an effort to become more aware of the situations and people who tend to set you down a tyrannical warpath. One way to create such awareness is to ask yourself some tough questions. Take time to reflect and answer the following questions:

1. In what situations am I most likely to lose composure and display explosive behaviors?

    a. With what kind of people? Those who I have power over in the moment, such as direct reports, customer service people, or even my kids?

    b. In what sorts of meetings or interactions? Is it when people disagree with me or challenge my ideas?

2. What are the initial symptoms that let me know that I am starting to lose control?

   a. Does my breathing change?

   b. Does my heart rate speed up?

   c. Do I have the urge to raise my voice, talk faster, or interrupt others?

   d. Do I start to feel antsy and fidgety? Do I find myself tapping the table, tapping my foot, or pacing?

Once you realize when the Tyrant is taking over, either because your colleague has given you feedback or you recognize some physical symptoms, you can start to work on strategies to control your behavior. Good techniques for calming yourself include controlling your breathing, taking a short break from a meeting or conversation, maintaining a friendly tone of voice, and speaking slowly.

Summary

There should be no assumption that a Tyrant's transformation will occur overnight or be sustained. For those who are extrinsically motivated, it is common to go back into their tyrannical comfort zone once they achieve what they want, such as a promotion, a bonus, or a more positive performance evaluation. Particularly for these types of individuals, it will be critical to ensure that the new behavior is sustained over a longer period of time, which will take serious ongoing effort. Working to develop intrinsic motivation should also be a part of their goals, because it will make them more likely to succeed in the long run.

With time, Tyrants should be able to develop their own coping mechanisms. If they continuously ask for feedback from people they trust, these people will be open and candid with them. Colleagues can give powerful insight into what's working to tame the inner Tyrant and what's not. Transformation might be a long and difficult road, but efforts will not go unrewarded.

CHAPTER THREE

THE USER AND ABUSER

User and Abuser leaders are natural takers in life. They believe they are entitled to the best option in any situation, whether or not it compromises the people or resources around them. A close relative of the Tyrant, they act selfishly and have the uncanny ability to bend other people's wills to get special treatment and favors. Through the use of charm and wit, many people feel unable to say no to Users and Abusers. When nice people go out of their way to help Users and Abusers, these takers in life don't offer the true appreciation that the people who help them deserve. In fact, they don't display gratitude because they believe deep down that they are entitled to special treatment and, furthermore, that others really want to help them and choose to do so. Even more interesting, Users and Abusers often lose respect over time for the people who serve and help them because they grow to believe that the helpers, which include most people they know, belong to a lower caste. Sound funny? Think twice and you will find many Users and Abusers in your life, I guarantee.

In the workplace, Users and Abusers cause an array of issues. From uneven work distribution to poor morale and burnout, when these leaders rise to the top, they certainly leave their mark.

What a User and Abuser Looks Like

Research shows that personality is a key determinant of people's ability or inability to behave in the workplace. Personality assessments capture aspects of personality that predict behavior. The Hogan Development Survey (HDS) assesses the dark side of personality, identifying toxic and nonproductive behaviors that can and often do derail careers. The table that follows identifies the three scales that a User and Abuser will typically score high on (7 or greater on a 10-point scale). Users and Abusers score high on the colorful, bold and mischievous scales. They act entitled to everything they get and use and abuse people to get what they want.

The User and Abuser's Leadershit Behaviors	
Three Highest *HDS Scores	How the User and Abuser will behave in the workplace based on *HDS scores
Colorful	Self-promoting, attention seeking, poor listening skills, easily distracted, manages by crisis, problems with being organized, may lack follow-through
Bold	Feedback resistant, overestimates talents and accomplishments, does not seek out options, demanding and overbearing, blames others, self-promoting, strong sense of entitlement, no sense of team loyalty
Mischievous	Makes intuitive not fact-based decisions, unwilling to follow others' rules, may not learn from past mistakes, takes, ill-advised risks without reviewing consequences, pushes the limits, ignores commitments, motivated by pleasure
Examples	Kim Jong-un or any dictator who uses people
*The Hogan Development Survey (HDS) evaluates the dark side of personality, identifying overused strengths and toxic assets that will derail careers if the behaviors are not kept in check.	

Evolution

Users and Abusers demonstrate this problematic behavior early in life. As children, they have a knack for convincing their siblings and friends to do things for them and they often have their parents wrapped around their little finger. As people agree to help Users and Abusers, it serves as positive reinforcement and encourages this behavior. Unless their behavior is changed early in life, they develop specific skills for using and abusing people; as they age they will only get better and better at it. When interacting with people who are natural givers or pleasers, the User and Abuser can turn into a monster.

For example, I have three daughters who have all been raised the same way. I noticed that one of my daughters demonstrated a User and Abuser tendency early in life. I noticed that instead of getting off of the couch to get a glass of water, she was more likely to ask her younger sister to do it. The younger girl, having a natural pleaser personality, would promptly respond to her sister's request by getting her a glass of water. When I confronted my older daughter, pointing out that she was using her younger sister by consistently asking her to go get water for her, she replied by saying that her sister actually enjoyed serving her. Yes, she used the word serving. From that day forward, the rule in my home has always been that each person gets her own glass of water and can't ask others to do so.

A Wolf in Sheep's Clothing

Users and Abusers thrive for two reasons:

Their behavior makes others question themselves and their duties; and

The way Users and Abusers ask for things is so natural, matter-of-fact, charming, and compelling that some people actually feel good about complying with the requests.

Jack experienced this in his first job after college, when he worked as a market analyst for an bicycle company. Jack received excellent feedback in his first annual performance review, but he wasn't given a pay increase. His manager and the department director told him that the company was having financial trouble and there was a freeze on pay increases. They both apologized and said they wished they could give him an increase.

After that meeting, Jack's boss pulled him aside and said he might have a good solution. He explained that he had an expense account that he used to buy supplies and then was reimbursed for the work expenses. Although he couldn't technically give Jack a raise, he could cover some of Jack's expenses if Jack submitted receipts. The only catch was that because Jack didn't actually have work expenses, his boss would be reimbursing him for personal expenses so it had to be their secret. Jack's boss said it was a sunk cost for the department, because if he didn't use it each quarter, it would go to waste anyway.

"I thought the arrangement sounded great," recounts Jack with a laugh. "My boss was helping me get the compensation he agreed I deserved even when the corporation couldn't. I trusted his judgment."

Jack decided to take his boss up on the offer and soon he started receiving personal checks from his boss. During the next year, Jack found himself slowly taking on more and more work while his boss spent more time busy with other important matters. Jack wondered if his boss had an ulterior motive for their financial arrangement. It seemed like Jack was working on projects that should have been his boss' responsibility and that his boss was taking credit for Jack's work. At first, Jack didn't mind. After all, his boss had gone out of his way to help him by generously sharing his expense account. This was Jack's first professional job, and he questioned whether that type of arrangement was common in the workplace.

"I really had no idea what to make of it," says Jack. "I remember telling some friends about the reimbursements and they thought it was strange, but positive. They said a lot of people have to do extra work for their bosses and they don't get paid extra so I should be happy."

Ultimately, Jack developed resentment for his boss, but it didn't last long, because the company declared bankruptcy soon after and ninety percent of the staff was laid off, including Jack, his boss, and the department manager.

What Can We Learn From This Story?

When employees start to realize they are being taken advantage of, they don't always speak up. Denial or fear of retaliation by the User and Abuser is enough to keep many employees quiet, especially if they have been put in a situation where they could also be seen as at fault. Users and Abusers have an uncanny way of roping others into their schemes to diffuse responsibility and blame should their behavior ever be questioned. Those who are being abused feel like they can't get help without personally getting in trouble.

So what should you do if you find yourself in this situation, especially if you report to a User and Abuser and they are more senior to you in the hierarchy?

Document every request and transaction from the User and Abuser.

Ask for a confidential conversation with Human Resources to check on company policies as well as your official duties and job description.

Ask former employees about their experience with Users and Abusers. They might even volunteer experiences with the User and Abuser you are trying to deal with. Senior Executives who demonstrate this type of behavior typically don't start late in life. You probably won't be surprised by what you will find out from their former employees or co-workers.

These three steps should give you the objective perspective needed to have a discussion about what is acceptable and what is not with the User and Abuser.

If the User and Abuser reports to you, you may want to address the issue by setting expectations and clearly describing the behaviors you will not tolerate. Be prepared to give specific examples of unacceptable behaviors (in particular) for User and Abusers who also present a low level of self-awareness.

This story shows that leaders who are Users and Abusers are especially negative role models for younger or less experienced employees who haven't developed a strong understanding of business ethics. After interactions with a User and Abuser, company policies and values may seem like casual suggestions rather than rules. Senior leaders should think hard before promoting Users and Abusers unless they want that mentality to become part of company culture.

Perception Matters

The issue of telling right from wrong isn't always black and white. Sometimes employees and companies can behave ethically, but achieve results that appear to be anything but ethical. The perception could be that the person was using and/ or abusing his or her power or role to get what he or she wanted, even if it was ethical and in the best interest of the company. That's why it's important for leaders to think about how other people would view a situation and outcome and take that into account when making decisions.

In my early career, I learned a hard lesson about how much perception matters. I was working for IBM to secure a huge sale when we ran into a major hardware installation problem. Part of the machine a client ordered got caught in the bureaucratic Brazilian customs department when it shipped from New York to Brazil. We had counted on that sale going through by the end of the year and this situation threatened to derail the plans of my entire team. I decided the only hope for getting the parts through customs quickly was to fly to Brasilia, the capital, and see what I could do in person. Because I'm Brazilian, I figured it would be easy to find whom I needed to talk to so that our case could be expedited. I didn't know anyone in customs nor did I have any government connections, but I was determined to get to the people in charge. They listened to me, realized the equipment and paperwork were okay and released it right away. I flew back to Rio de Janeiro, expecting my boss to be overjoyed; the sale would count for that calendar year. It also meant that no one would have to work overtime during the holidays to fix the issue. Instead, he was furious. He said that it didn't matter if I had resolved the issue in an ethical way; it would certainly look like the company had bribed someone. His words were clear, "Just being honest is not enough; having the perception of honesty is equally important."

I was dumbfounded, but I never forgot his words. Being so focused on fixing the problem as quickly as possible, I hadn't thought about what people would think if I succeeded. Because the chances of expediting and resolving an issue with customs by talking it out seemed slim to none, no one would believe we had actually done it. They would think I was a User and Abuser, whether or not it was actually true. It was a powerful lesson: sometimes actions aren't ethically wrong, but if they can be perceived as wrong, those actions are probably not a good choice.

Years later, when I was a manager, a team member who reported to me developed a business case to justify expensing a bicycle to the company. He was staffed on a two-year project in Houston. His justification was that it was faster and more cost effective for him to ride a bike to the client instead of taking cabs every day or renting a car. He showed how the price of the bike corresponded to the cost of taking cabs for six months. After six months, his plan would actually generate cost savings for the organization. The math was bulletproof and his case was sound and logical.

At that time, my old boss' words came vividly to my mind: "Just being honest is not enough; having the perception of honesty is equally important." I explained to my associate that I would not approve the expense even though he had a sound and logical case. When people would see that he expensed a bike and I approved that expense, nobody would care what the context or business case was; it wouldn't seem right or honest.

Making Room for Innovation

When managing a perception of fairness and doing the right thing are the main factors for making a decision, it can sometimes feel like you're settling for a second-rate decision. In these situations, you may want to think about whether a widespread change in policy would be appropriate. That way, you aren't making exceptions for individual people; you are making a potentially better option available to everyone.

As an extreme example, if you learn that incorporating bicycles into the company's travel expenses policy could save money in the long term – not to mention improving employees exercising and health — you could gauge employees' interest in whether they would prefer riding a bicycle. Depending on the response, your organization could adjust the allocation of future travel funds and purchase bicycles employees could use. Not only would it be a smart financial decision, it could positively impact employee engagement and organizational culture. In supporting outside-of-the-box policy changes, senior leaders could show they are open to employees' ideas, and embrace innovation.

A Culture of Abuse

Unfortunately, sometimes using and abusing employees is the cultural norm rather than the exception. In many organizations, salaried employees are expected to regularly work unhealthy, long hours, and be on call when they are away from the office. They may also be expected to cancel requested vacation days to work on an urgent project and/or are expected to work during their vacation.

For example, some organizations that offer professional services are prone to developing a culture where abuse throughout the ranks is common. Employees are often rewarded for billing as many hours as they possibly can, even though they aren't paid on an hourly basis or compensated for overtime. To make the problem worse, partners or executives bid on projects and often quote fewer hours than it will take to do the work. This undercuts the competition without lowering the firm's hourly rate and makes partners look good by bringing in more business. However, it puts employees in a situation where they are expected to do more with fewer resources and not bill all of the time they actually worked on a particular project. This creates a conflict for employees because one of the key criteria for being promoted is high billable hours and utilization, but in order to make partners look good and deliver profitable projects, junior people are pressured to report lower hours than they worked. Leaders know this happens, but many aren't sympathetic to newer employees' lack of work-life balance, and view it as a rite of passage. Such an attitude creates a white-collar sweatshop.

Because a culture of abuse is so widespread in certain organizations, digging out of this leadershit may seem impossible. Employees show their disdain through turnover, but even if these organizations retain workers, the culture typically stays the same.

What Can We Learn From This Story?

As an employee, if you are given an assignment that cannot be completed in the number of hours your boss requests, let your boss know, and document it in an email. Also document the unbilled or unassigned hours you work every week. The same holds true for projects with an unreasonable deadline. If you or your team members need to work 12-hour days to meet a deadline, keep your boss in the loop via email. If you're asked to work when you're on vacation, keep a log of the requests as well as the dates and hours you worked.

When you get the chance to complete an upward appraisal or employee survey, make it known that you have regularly been working extremely long hours. If your manager has been underestimating the necessary hours to complete projects and it's causing the team to be overworked, speak up. If you have been expected to attend meetings or work during vacation, report this.

Employees are often hesitant to speak up because they are afraid to make waves. However, employee surveys that are kept confidential are an opportunity for victims of Users and Abusers to articulate how they feel about the abuse. Senior Executives will see this feedback and have an opportunity to coach managers or partners about how they manage client projects and direct reports. Depending on the outcome of the surveys, it will become clear whether the behavioral issue is one or a couple of individuals, or whether there is a culture that nurtures Users and Abusers. Human Resources should be informed if employees have been told to work when they're on vacation—this is an employment law issue that leaves companies liable for lawsuits. Turning around a culture of abuse doesn't happen overnight, but it will happen if enough people decide to speak up and management decides to take appropriate action on the problem.

Being Used by Prospective Clients

Due to the fierce competitive environment most companies face these days, service providers can find themselves walking a fine line between delivering more than expected and giving away too much for too little compensation. They do this as a way of strengthening relationships and loyalty. However, this creates a fertile ground for a User and Abuser prospect or client.

You're probably familiar with how it starts. Someone outside of your company asks if they can pick your brain about your area of expertise. You think this could be a perfect opportunity to showcase your knowledge and demonstrate your commitment. So you agree, but you soon learn the brain-picker isn't interested or ready to move forward with a formal relationship, paid project, or engagement. When they ask you for more advice, you think you're that much closer to getting the contract but it still doesn't pan out.

If this sounds familiar, you know that you are being used and abused. You have been providing guidance and essentially working for free. It may not be a big deal at first: 10 minutes here, 30 minutes for coffee there, but it adds up.

Somewhere down the road, you decide you've had enough. You need to speak with this User and Abuser about the value of your time. However, you aren't quite sure how much of your time you've already given away for free. This ambiguity makes it harder to know where to draw the line.

The lesson? Log all of your time spent helping people outside of your company, even if you don't have a formal relationship or engagement with them. When you document your time, it will be easier to see how much value you have provided to others. You will be able to speak up sooner when you notice certain people taking advantage of you. When someone crosses the threshold of using too much of your time without paying for it, you initiate a conversation:

"I've enjoyed helping you during the past month and learning about your business. I've noticed that I've spent X hours working with you and this level of support is starting to feel like a project. Since my schedule is so busy, I would be happy to offer you a retainer for my services where I would set aside X hours/days a month to help you. Given the amount of support you've needed in the past month, I think that amount of time would be a good fit for both of us."

Being Used by Clients

If a current client starts to require more support than they agreed to pay for, you might need to revisit the project scope and deliverables. Scope creep is common in professional services and it's often unintentional. It is often difficult for clients to gauge the support they will need before a project is under way. Therefore service providers need to recognize when plans for completing an assignment should be adjusted. Having a candid conversation about this right away can resolve the situation. Waiting until a project is significantly out-of-scope is problematic because your client has developed expectations of what you will deliver for a certain fee.

A good strategy for managing scope creep is to let clients know if any work you are doing is outside of the project plan, even if you're willing to throw it in as a freebie in the beginning. Send an email to document this conversation so you can refer back to it, if needed:

"In the interest of making sure you're pleased with this project, we are happy to take care of this request even though it's outside of the scope. If you need more assistance of this nature moving forward, we will need to discuss updating our agreement to reflect the additional work."

This strategy is two-fold; you will look generous from the onset of the relationship by delivering extra value, and clients are reminded of the project's boundaries without you having to tell them no.

Summary

User and Abuser leaders are challenging to work for, but it's possible to avoid succumbing to their every wish. The key is to keep an eye out for the red flags described in this chapter so you can identify situations that have a high potential for becoming abusive. Instead of worrying about being nice and cooperative, focus on not allowing yourself and your colleagues to be manipulated.

CHAPTER FOUR

THE MANIPULATOR

The Netflix TV drama *House of Cards* has gained a passionate following, shocking viewers in every episode by the lengths the main character, Frank Underwood, will go to gain power. On his journey up the political ladder, we've seen him lie, cheat, steal, and even kill to get what he wants. The motives that drive his behavior are sometimes unclear because he is thinking steps ahead of his current situation. He is a master manipulator and uses the people around him in any way he can to get what he wants. As a TV character, he is a train wreck; appalling and horrifying in a manner that makes us unable to look away. We wonder if there are really people out there in the world who are as manipulative and deceitful as Frank Underwood. As it turns out, the truth is often stranger than fiction.

Manipulation is a particularly slippery type of leadershit. Unlike other culprits who exhibit obvious leadership shortcomings, such as the Poor Communicator or the Unaccountable, the Manipulator is a master of deception. The No-Filter operates in secrecy and can only thrive when his true nature remains hidden. The Manipulator is calculating and shapes the people and world around him to get what he wants. More often than not, if people realize that they have been manipulated, it will be too late to reverse the consequences and results.

Chances are you've been manipulated countless times throughout your life, and most times, you didn't suspect a thing. This chapter uncovers the most common forms of workplace manipulation, hopefully, making it easier to identify when you are being used as a pawn in the Manipulator's game.

What a Manipulator Looks Like

Research shows that personality is a key determinant of people's ability or inability to behave in the workplace. Personality assessments capture aspects of personality that predict behavior. The Hogan Development Survey (HDS) assesses the dark side of personality, identifying toxic and nonproductive behaviors that can and do derail careers. The table that follows identifies the three HDS scales that a Manipulator will typically score high on (7 or greater on a 10-point scale). The Manipulator's behavior is seen as mischievous, cautious, and skeptical. They are individuals who interact easily with people, but pit people against each other. They may also be seen as dishonest.

The Manipulator's Leadershit Behaviors	
Three Highest *HDS Scores	How the Manipulator will behave in the workplace based on *HDS scores
Mischievous	Makes intuitive not fact-based decisions, unwilling to follow others' rules, may not learn from past mistakes, takes, ill-advised risks without reviewing consequences, pushes the limits, ignores commitments, motivated by pleasure
Cautious	Slow to make decisions, resistant to change, reluctant to take chances, motivated not to fail, unassertive, conservative, perceived as holding others back.
Skeptical	Sensitive to criticism, argumentative, critical, defensive, easily angered, suspicious of others' intentions, prone to fault-finding
Examples	Frank Underwood in television series House of Cards
*The Hogan Development Survey (HDS) evaluates the dark side of personality, identifying overused strengths and toxic assets that will derail careers if the behaviors are not kept in check.	

The Opportunist

Manipulators recognize when situations could be spun to reap more personal benefits. Opportunists not only manipulate people, they work the system to get what they want. Any lack of clarity or ambiguity is seen as an opportunity to do whatever they want. As children, they caused many parents to fight because their selective hearing led them to believe one parent gave them permission to do something, even if the other parent clearly forbid it. As adults in the workplace, opportunists initiate projects, approve expenditures, and take actions without getting official approval; then claim they thought it was acceptable or compliant with policy. They thrive in chaotic and disorganized environments because it makes it easier to get away with things. Opportunists often claim a creative or entrepreneurial personality to justify their perspective and behavior.

How to deal with opportunists:

☐ If you have opportunists in your team, you are at risk of having them interpret your words in a way that is most convenient and advantageous for them. Make sure your directions and expectations are unequivocally clear and make yourself available to answer questions.

☐ As a senior leader, it's in your best interest to make company policies thorough and detailed. In addition, you may want to review these with your team to clarify any confusion. Know that any gray area can be taken advantage of without technically being a violation.

The Eternal Victim

Playing the victim is a sneaky way Manipulators use people's emotions to get what they want. The eternal victim leverages misfortunes to augment situations and take advantage of the system. Eternal victims are highly skilled at garnering sympathy from others, which often leads to special treatment. They use excuses to explain why they weren't able to meet expectations or requirements, and in the process, actually make others feel sorry for them. At the office, these are the people who just seem to have bad luck. They are plagued by car trouble that prevents them from being punctual; all of their deadlines seem to fall on the same day, making it impossible to get things done; their computer or email account doesn't work properly, which hinders their productivity. Health issues are often embellished and broadcast such that a simple cold is portrayed as an incapacitating disability. You name it, the eternal victim has experienced it. People who are highly empathetic and make decisions based on feelings need to be acutely aware of eternal victims or risk being manipulated by them.

Recently, I was told the story about a woman named Kim who was fired and rehired by playing the role of a victim. Kim was let go for performance reasons because her employer finally saw through all of her excuses. After being terminated, she contacted a major client of her former employer, crying and explaining how she would no longer be working on their project. Kim spun such a good yarn that the client became irate. Kim told them that she had been fired after a series of personal misfortunes that had temporarily affected her work. The client threatened to pull all of their business from the company based on how cruel the company was to a loyal employee. Kim's CEO had his back against the wall and had no choice but to rehire her.

How to Deal with Eternal Victims

Knowing when to be compassionate and when to put your foot down is tricky. No one wants to be unsympathetic and cold-hearted, but no one wants to be manipulated, either. If you notice a pattern and think you have an eternal victim on your hands, as a best practice, document every time that person misses a deadline or falls short of an obligation. Whether it's a direct report, a co-worker, or a manager, keep notes on file that you can refer to later. If you document through email, you will have evidence of addressing the issues.

☐ If the culprit is a direct report, you should initiate a conversation before the situation escalates. Tell the person that you understand everyone goes through tough situations, but you're noticing a troubling pattern. When you share your documentation, it will be clear that violations are kept on record, which is kryptonite to the Manipulator. He or she will be faced with the choice of ending the victim pattern, or finding another job that allows for more leeway. For you, it's a win-win.

☐ If the eternal victim is your co-worker, you should discuss the situation with your manager or human resources director. Providing facts and examples will support your case and make it easier for them to help you.

☐ If the victim is your boss, that's certainly a more difficult situation and you are in a tough spot. He will likely use a number of different excuses to dump his work on you. If that is the case, you can ask your boss for help reprioritizing tasks so that you can deliver on the most important ones. Bring him into a problem-solving mode with you and perhaps he will realize dumping his work on you is not the solution to all of his troubles.

☐ If your boss is not responsive to your efforts to end the manipulation, you can and should seek assistance or advice from a Human Resource professional.

The Puppet Master

This type of Manipulator is strategic when it comes to influencing people. They interact easily with people and know how to cater to different people to get what they want. First, they quickly understand people's motives, agendas, and hot buttons. Then, they morph into different personas like chameleons and play whatever role is required to get people to act and react in a way that fits their needs. They excel at getting coworkers to trust them while eroding the trust their coworkers have in one another. As the most damaging form of manipulation, Puppet Masters work behind the scenes making people think or do certain things to shape situations without bringing attention to themselves.

Meet Mike, the boss, who wanted to get rid of John, an employee in his team, but didn't want to be viewed as the bad cop. For several months, Mike closely observed his team, gaining a better understanding of who got along with whom and who couldn't work together. Even though John was liked by most of his colleagues, he and Julie didn't see eye-to-eye on a number of issues. Mike saw this as an opportunity to get rid of John. He changed the structure of his team and promoted Julie, giving her a couple of his direct reports, including John. Mike then told Julie that John didn't seem to respect her and that she had his permission to take action whenever she felt it was appropriate. Even though John and Julie didn't have a history of working well together, John had never shown the disrespect for Julie that Mike stated. Nevertheless, all it took was a few disagreements between John and Julie for her to pull the trigger and fire John. In the end, Mike got what he wanted but came out of the situation smelling like a rose.

Puppet Masters understand organizational dynamics. Astute and deliberate communicators, they are calculating and rarely make communication mistakes. To avoid conflict, they pretend to agree with people, but move forward and do whatever they want. They intentionally, but subtly, misrepresent what people say, pitting coworkers against one another. They block communication between parties to create dissent and divide and conquer. A form of soft bullying, manipulation gets people to do or accept things that they normally wouldn't. Think about Machiavelli's book *The Prince*: "the end justifies the means" or "where the willingness is great, the difficulties cannot be great." In the Puppet Master's mind whatever he wants to accomplish is so important that it offsets any manipulative tactics used to achieve his goals. That's why these people are often referred to as Machiavellian. In many ways, Puppet Masters are cowards because they get other people to say or do the things they are afraid of doing.

How to Deal with Puppet Masters

- ☐ Inclusiveness is the Puppet Master's enemy. If colleagues have frequent and open communication, it is more difficult for manipulation to occur. Holding more group meetings and having fewer one-on-one interactions can defeat the Puppet Master. By gathering all parties involved in the same room, you create a high level of exposure. This makes it risky and difficult for them to pit people against one another or misrepresent what has been said.

- ☐ Because Puppet Masters thrive on confidentiality, documenting conversations helps to keep them in check. If a Puppet Master talks to you in private, follow it up with an email to document the conversation. Having the email on record is enough to prove the conversation occurred. If companies have a culture where everything is documented, Manipulators can't survive for long.

How to Know When You're Being Manipulated

With so many kinds of manipulation there are many ways to be taken advantage of. Here are a few signs to watch for in the workplace:

- ☐ You and your coworkers hear different things about the same topic from the same person.

- ☐ A colleague refuses to document something.

- ☐ A colleague refuses to show documentation to support something he or she says is true.

☐   A process suddenly becomes bureaucratic and you
    are blocked from doing something that was once
    easy to do.

When You Can't Beat Them, Try Negotiating

I recently spoke with a woman who told me an appalling story
of being manipulated by her own board. Irina came to the
U.S. from a former Soviet Union country as a political refugee,
many years ago, when she was quite young. Being smart and
hardworking, she got a job in the financial services industry,
and rose through the ranks to ultimately become the president
of a small bank. During the first ten years of her trajectory, she
worked nonstop to make the unprofitable business turn into
a profitable one, which was no small feat. Soon after she was
promoted to president, an investor in the bank made it known
that he wanted someone else in charge. Little by little, through
increasing investments in the bank, he worked the board and
stripped Irina of her responsibilities. He told the board that
he was aware that she was burning out and needed to be
released of some of her duties. The investor was manipulating
the board by leading them to believe that Irina was burned out
and stressed out, and, therefore no longer capable of running
a fast growing business. With board support, he soon put
one of his professional connections and a long time protégé
in Irina's place. The board had interpreted Irina's somewhat
emotional protests over being disempowered as evidence of
stress and inability to handle the high-pressure situation. Given
Irina's stellar performance, the board's reason for removing
her was not performance, but based on her need for some
time off. Irina felt like she was being discriminated against,
so she approached the investor to ask him why she was being
demoted. Before Irina even had a chance to mention a potential
case of discrimination, the investor told her he knew what she
was thinking and she should not try to sue him or the bank. He
told her that he was wealthy and would be happy to spend a
huge chunk of money to crush her in court. Manipulators often

resort to threats to ensure that they are protected, and this is exactly what the major investor did.

Unable to get a direct line to the board, Irina thought about her situation and agonized over what she should do. She knew the investor was in the wrong and that what he was doing could put him in a liable situation. But she also knew his threat should be taken seriously and that it was likely he would win if they went to court. She decided her best option was to move on to another job, but now that her title change showed a demotion, she was concerned about the implication of the demotion to future job prospects. Irina decided to negotiate with the investor. She told him that if he gave her a higher title, she would start looking for another position; she wouldn't sue him and/or cause bad publicity. He agreed and gave her the title of Chairman, which came with a few day-to-day and operational responsibilities. This gave her the status she needed to apply to top positions in her industry.

Irina eventually landed another president role in an even larger institution, given her career success track and her promotion to Chairman. She now has a fabulous board and professional investors who treat her with respect. She is a clear example of somebody who beat a manipulator at his own game.

What Can We Learn From This Story?

In situations where you're backed into a corner and the Manipulator's true identity has been revealed to you, negotiating might be the smartest career move. Irina didn't feel like a grueling, expensive lawsuit would be a win for her personally or professionally, whether or not she won the case. With that in mind, finding a new job as quickly as possible became her goal. By negotiating with the Manipulator, she came out of the situation with a more executive title that helped her ultimately get a better job.

Don't get me wrong, it doesn't feel good to negotiate with someone who doesn't deserve the time of day, but if you aren't willing to sacrifice for yourself and your career to fight the Manipulator for justice, negotiating could be your best option.

Summary

Even though people at the top of the food chain are most frequently pegged for manipulation, it's often found a few rungs lower on the ladder. Once it has spread throughout the organization, it really becomes part of the culture and thrives in power positions because very few people will dare to confront them when they are playing others or the system. However, most don't need the highest level in an organization to achieve their goals; Manipulators can and do operate at any level.

Because most Manipulators play the same game, there generally isn't room for too many of them within the same organization. When a company has a plethora of Manipulators, its culture becomes incredibly political. The workplace turns into a game of who can outsmart who. This type of environment is unpleasant, unproductive, and toxic. It should be avoided at all costs. The goal is to limit the amount of manipulation in the workplace.

Most Manipulators can be spotted. After they are exposed, it is more difficult for them to use their power for evil. On the other hand, expert Manipulators typically don't get caught; they weasel their way out of every situation, often choosing to leave the organization if the risk of exposure becomes too high.

Thinking back to *House of Cards*, Frank Underwood's hunger for power threatens his ability to use manipulation effectively. This goes to show that even the most skilled manipulators can't keep fooling everyone all of the time. Remember Abraham Lincoln's famous quote: "You can fool all the people some of the time and some of the people all the time, but you cannot fool all the people all the time." At some point, life-long Manipulators lose the support and the power they so value.

CHAPTER FIVE

THE CHAMELEON

Like their namesake, Chameleon leaders change their colors depending on the situation. They are often difficult to spot in the office because they work hard to blend into their surroundings. Although you might not notice them at first, they certainly notice you. Keen observers of organizational dynamics, Chameleons sit back and take it all in before they make a move. They are conservative in articulating their position or making decisions because they prefer to be on the popular or winning side of any debate. As such, they wait to see which way the wind will blow on various topics. If they pick a side that starts to become less popular, they will flip-flop to the new, winning side.

This behavior is not only confusing and irritating to others in the workplace, it's highly unproductive. A leader's inability to proactively make decisions and stick to them causes unnecessary back-and-forth communication, and delays progress. At best, coworkers see Chameleon leaders as wishy-washy; at worst, sneaky and deceitful.

What a Chameleon Looks Like

Research shows that personality is a key determinant of people's ability or inability to behave in the workplace. Personality assessments capture aspects of personality that predict behavior. The Hogan Development Survey (HDS) assesses the dark side of personality, identifying toxic and nonproductive behaviors that can and do derail careers. The table that follows identifies the three HDS scales that

The Chameleon's Leadershit Behaviors	
Three Highest *HDS Scores	How the Chameleon will behave in the workplace based on *HDS scores
Dutiful	Compliant, reluctant to make decisions, unwilling to challenge the status quo, withdraw from politically charged situations, conforming, strong desire to please others, may not stand up for subordinates.
Cautious	Slow to make decisions, resistant to change, reluctant to take chances, motivated not to fail, unassertive, conservative, perceived as holding others back.
Reserved	Interpersonally insensitive, preference for working alone, uncomfortable around strangers, uncommunicative, feedback deficient, reserved, not a team player
Examples	Charles de Gaulle, French President during World War II
*The Hogan Development Survey (HDS) evaluates the dark side of personality, identifying overused strengths and toxic assets that will derail careers if the behaviors are not kept in check.	

a Chameleon will typically score high on (7 or greater on a 10-point scale). The Chameleon is seen as dutiful, cautious, and reserved. They are individuals who are politically correct, risk-adverse and don't like to take a position on anything.

Lucy had been a manager at a mid-sized consulting firm for two years when Jan became her new boss, a senior VP of marketing. Lucy liked Jan, but suddenly didn't understand what was expected of her and her direct reports. Jan frequently gave conflicting instructions. The direct mail campaign that Jan said was so important for Lucy's team was put on hold for a new design project. The next day when Lucy mentioned the new design project to her team, a direct report told her that Jan said they should focus on a public relations program. Now the marketing team had a plethora of unfinished projects and difficulty prioritizing even the simplest tasks. The team emailed Jan for clarification, but found it hard to get answers because Jan was busy traveling to client meetings.

Lucy and her colleagues figured Jan might be having trouble prioritizing because she was new to her role and still learning about the company. However, after several confusing months of repeatedly starting and stopping new projects based on Jan's changing whims, the marketing team and senior leaders realized Jan was a Chameleon. She was so busy trying to look good that she was more concerned with pleasing people and doing what they suggested rather than making her own decisions to guide her team.

Species Origin and Evolution

Chameleon behavior typically starts at a young age, when friends heavily influence children and young adults. If you have children, you know how quickly they can change their minds about what's in. Things they like go from incredibly cool to embarrassingly uncool overnight based on opinions from their peers and social media. Even though it is hard to keep up with their lightning-fast changes in opinion, it's easy to understand why they're so fickle; everyone wants to be liked and fit in somewhere. Agreeing with people creates a harmonious situation in the short term, and that feels good. That's why kids follow suit when their friends jump from trend to trend. This hot-cold behavior is normal for young people, but when adults behave this way in the workplace, it's a case of Chameleon leadershit.

Adults develop a sense of who they are and what's important. Core beliefs help people analyze situations and guide decision-making. In most situations, once adults know the facts, they form an opinion. Sometimes that opinion can waver if they hear another perspective, but most people don't flip-flop back and forth on a regular basis.

If a coworker has a markedly harder time making decisions, it is noticeable. People wonder what's happening. Why is the person so confused? Is she struggling with her values or the decision? Because it is a complex situation, co-workers may not recognize the Chameleon behavior at first and give it a pass. However, when the behavior becomes a pattern, the Chameleon is pegged as a flake who can't make up his mind. However, sometimes the behavior is interpreted as intentionally misleading others. Either may be the case, and neither is good.

Habitat

Chameleons thrive in environments where there is a lot of conflict. Conflict often exists during mergers and acquisitions and is present in companies that employ a high percentage of assertive, decisive employees. This culture gives Chameleons something legitimate to work with. When their colleagues have strong and conflicting opinions, Chameleons can hold back, staying out of the drama until a winning side emerges that they can support. Chameleons can also easily step into a valuable and thoughtful mediator role—the peacemaker role brings disagreeing employees to their senses and a common ground. However, the longevity of this role is only valuable in environments that have frequent, deep, and long-term conflicts.

Some are aware of their lizard-like tendencies and use them as a way to navigate office politics; others act this way unintentionally.

In more cohesive working environments, Chameleons try to bring peace to situations that are already functional. They stay neutral and try to please others, and as a result, fewer decisions get made and progress slows down. In this environment, Chameleons are easier to identify.

How to Spot a Chameleon in the Wild

Chameleons are motivated by:

- [ ] Wanting to please others

- [ ] Being afraid to stand up for themselves

- [ ] Gaining power and influence

Chameleons behave in ways that align with these motivations. Some are aware of their lizard-like tendencies and use them as a way to navigate office politics; others act this way unintentionally.

Chameleons are easily identified in meetings or group settings by the following behaviors:

- [ ] They avoid speaking first—they wait to see where everyone else stands before they contribute to a conversation.

- [ ] They want to be seen as the peacemaker—if a debate gets heated, they will often take a mediator role, hoping to add value and create harmony.

- [ ] They often vote with the majority—if Chameleons have to vote or make a decision they will wait to see where everyone else stands before committing.

- [ ] They defer to powerful people—when they are able to withhold their comments until the end of a discussion, they will agree or defer to the most powerful or senior people in the room.

Chameleons are more difficult to spot when they are your boss, because you often don't have access to key meetings. In meetings, Chameleon leaders may agree with their direct reports on a matter, but come back later with a different decision or direction. It's not always possible to know what caused the change in direction. Chameleon leaders might meet with their boss and never share the point-of-view they agreed on with their direct reports. Instead, they wait for their boss to provide an opinion and agree with that. Then they return to the team and let them know that there has been a change of plans. As a direct report, this is a situation where you wish you could be a fly on the wall to witness the conversation your boss has with her superior. However, without witnessing the conversation, it's difficult to know how things played out. Just like in the previous story of Jan, the marketing SVP, if your boss regularly comes back to the team with a new perspective and plan to move forward, it's likely you are in the hands of a Chameleon.

How to Discourage Color Changes

If you work with a Chameleon, there are steps you can take to reduce the frequency of color changes.

Direct Reports

If Chameleons report to you, have a clear and direct conversation about their behavior, explaining how and why it is damaging to workplace productivity and career success. During this conversation, touch on the following points:

- Encourage them to add value from their experience and expertise and share their point of view:

    o This is especially valuable for young employees who are learning to be professional. Young staffers often feel comfortable agreeing with the most powerful person in the room; they need to understand that they add value by sharing their expertise and experience. This allows them to develop and share an educated perspective to situations that would benefit from more insight.

- Clarify that their suggestions or recommendations won't always end up being the best option. No one is correct all of the time.

- It is okay to take risks and have a unique position, provided you have logical and fact-based reasons to support it. It's not always possible to predict the best recommendation, but an informed one is a good contribution.

☐ Tell them not to waver based on where others stand.

- People notice and don't respect it when colleagues flip-flop on issues. Chameleons are often unaware of how they are perceived by others, so explain this directly.

☐ Suggest they join the discussion and refrain from facilitating.

- Long-time Chameleons are comfortable stepping into this role, especially if they have experience working in advisory or consulting positions. Remind your direct reports that having an insightful point- of-view is more valuable than guiding others to share their views.

Peers and Senior Leaders

If the Chameleon is at your level or higher, it is more difficult to address the behavior directly. Candid conversations are obviously ideal, but not always possible without risking damage to the relationship or to your career. Instead, try the following to help Chameleons make decisions on their own.

☐ Document all conversations.

☐ When Chameleons give their opinions or say they will do something, document it. If you speak in person, send a follow-up email that details the topic, the opinions shared, and promises made. Identify agreed-upon next steps and be specific. This should hold Chameleons accountable. If you can copy another team member, this works even better.

☐ When a decision is needed, give Chameleons time to think.

   o Chameleons want to consider all of the facts before taking a stance. Plan to meet a week before you need a decision so they have time to consider options. Make it clear that you expect Chameleons to come to the next meeting equipped with their own point of view. This encourages a more informed and thoughtful approach.

☐ In situations that require a vote and everyone knows the options, ask Chameleons to vote first. Don't let them pass, either.

☐ For important and difficult meetings, use a professional facilitator; this prevents Chameleons from taking this role.

☐ Talk to your Human Resources Director. They may be able to talk to Chameleons or the Chameleon's boss. Better yet, the Human Resources Director might recommend trying a 360 evaluation to uncover feedback that would help.

☐ When a Chameleon is a peer and avoids giving his opinion, tell him you need him to take a position for efficiency and clarity.

Lifespan and Longevity

Whether an organization is rife with conflict or not, Chameleons rarely rise to top leadership positions because executives tend to see them as weak and ineffective. Chameleons gain a reputation for not having control because they are so easily influenced; direct reports know what buttons to push to get what they want. Like puppets or talking heads, Chameleons may hold a position of authority, but employees behind the scenes guide their every move.

I worked with an organization where a senior leader was so easily influenced by his direct reports that their strategy was to be the last person he spoke to before he made an important decision. One time they even invited him over for dinner to wine and dine him the night before a decision deadline. This kind of leader isn't typically the best candidate to run an organization.

Even though it is rare, C-Suite Chameleons exist. However, most often their careers stall before they get anywhere near the top. Why? Great leaders know there is simply no value in employing someone who always agrees with them. Yes-Men are seen as suck-ups who can't be trusted. Tyrants are particularly incompatible with Chameleons. Although they will use Chameleons to reinforce their agendas and do their dirty work, they don't respect Chameleons and view them as a waste of time and money. Conversely, Tyrants intimidate Chameleons and bring out their best lizard-like behavior. Because Tyrants often rise fairly far up the corporate ladder, they become roadblocks in Chameleons' career paths.

Chameleons have trouble relating to their peers and earning their respect. As an example, I worked with a woman named Sarah, who exhibited Chameleon-like behaviors. Trust me, it didn't go unnoticed by coworkers. After two years, she had a reputation for being a wishy-washy pushover and a brown-noser. Tenured employees warned new-hires about Sarah's inability to make decisions so they would be better prepared to work with her. It was unfortunate. She was so focused on avoiding conflict and staying in everyone's good graces that her behavior had a negative effect on her career. People didn't respect Sarah or think she was capable of taking on more responsibility because she never had her own opinions about anything.

Are You a Chameleon?

If you notice these behaviors in yourself, you should first determine the cause. Consider the following:

- Fear of going against the powers that be

    - Think about the three motivating factors—pleasing others, being afraid to stand up for yourself, and gaining power and influence. If any of these situations are influencing you, ask yourself what kind of leader you want to be—Do you want to be courageous or weak? Don't let fear hold you back from doing what you think is right. If you can't get past the fear and/or politics, you might want to reconsider the cultural fit between you and your employer.

- Unsure of the best position or decision in a complex situation

    - People's opinions waver when they really aren't sure of the right position. For example, you might see pluses and minuses to several options. When this happens, you should join in the discussion, articulating the alternatives, respective benefits, risks, and potential implications. More often than not, this process will help you make a decision on what you think is best. At some point, though, you have to take a position and remain with it. You owe it to your employees, colleagues, and business, even if you can see both sides of the coin.

☐ The issue doesn't seem relevant or important to you

  o Sometimes, people really don't have an
     opinion because they either see all options as
     equal, or they just don't think the issue on the
     table is important enough to chime into the
     discussion. When that's the case, be honest
     and say that in this particular debate you just
     don't care. Say that and get out of the way,
     allowing others to make the decision and
     move on. Don't step into the facilitator role
     to give the impression that you are engaged.
     SImilarly, if you were previously unsure of
     the best position, but now see the options as
     equal, tell your colleagues you could support
     either alternative because the expected net
     results look like a wash to you.

Summary

On the Leadershit spectrum, Chameleons are seen as
particularly spineless, garnering little respect from colleagues
at all levels. However, while they exhibit unproductive and
unhealthy behaviors, they don't typically have malicious
intentions and they aren't out to hurt anyone. Sometimes
they act selfishly to further their own careers, but that is as
intentional as their Leadershit gets.

I encourage you to use the tips in this chapter to help yourself
or a Chameleon colleague gain self-awareness and the ability
to change. In doing so, you will make a positive impact on that
person's life or your own life as well as your workplace culture.

CHAPTER SIX

THE NO-FILTER

Mouths that move faster than their brains plague no-Filter leaders. They are the first to talk in meetings; they speak out of turn and often find a foot in their mouths. Extroverted and impulsive, these people say what they're thinking before considering how their audiences will receive it. Often described as a loose cannons, No-Filters have unpredictable responses and behaviors that shock, entertain, and annoy both colleagues and customers alike.

The opposite of the Chameleon, the No-Filter *always* has a point of view and is bursting at the seams to make it known. Unfortunately, No-Filters don't think about the implications or potential impact of their words, often spurting out half-baked thoughts that offend others and waste people's time. No-Filters crave attention and achieve it by inappropriately dominating conversations through any means necessary.

Even though No-Filters' offensive behaviors are often just mildly annoying, in extreme situations, they can cause irreparable damage to a company's reputation or even spark a lawsuit.

What a No-Filter Leader Looks Like

Research shows that personality is a key determinant of people's ability or inability to behave in the workplace. Personality assessments capture aspects of personality that predict behavior. The Hogan Development Survey (HDS) assesses the dark side of personality, identifying toxic and nonproductive behaviors that can and do derail careers. The table that follows identifies the three HDS scales that a No-Filter will typically score high on (7 or greater on a 10-point scale). A No-Filter's behavior is seen as leisurely, mischievous and colorful. These individuals are extroverted and impulsive and draw attention to themselves as much as possible. Their behavior is inappropriate with mild to severe consequences.

No-Filter Moments

We have all had our No-Filter Moments. Chances are each one of us can think back to when we said something that made others (and us) cringe. That's a good sign because it means we are aware of what we said and why it was inappropriate.

The No-Filter's Leadershit Behaviors	
Three Highest *HDS Scores	How the No-Filter will behave in the workplace based on *HDS scores
Leisurely	Seemingly cooperative, unwilling to confront others, doesn't understand sense of urgency, passive resistance, works on own timetable, hard to coach, stubborn, procrastinates when performing uninteresting work.
Mischievous	Makes intuitive (not data-base) decisions, unwilling to follow others' rules, may not learn from past mistakes, takes risks without reviewing consequences, pushes the limits, ignores commitments, motivated by pleasure.
Colorful	Self-promoting, attention seeking, poor listening skills, easily distracted, manages by crisis, problems with organization, lacks follow-through
Examples	Al Gore, Robin Williams, Silvio Berlusconi (complimented President Obama on his suntan, for example)
*The Hogan Development Survey (HDS) evaluates the dark side of personality, identifying overused strengths and toxic assets that will derail careers if the behaviors are not kept in check.	

No-Filter Moments are particularly bad for celebrities and politicians. Instead of their verbal blunders disappearing in a few seconds, they live on for eternity in the media. This chapter features these moments, showing why it's important to think before talking. We also discuss how to handle No-Filters and what to do if you find yourself occasionally being one yourself.

Understanding the No-Filter's Motivation

There are three types of No-Filters: 1) Offensive and Rude; 2) Offbeat and Irrelevant; 3) The No-Filter by Choice. Each is distinguished primarily by their behavior--those who can't help themselves and those who take pride in their behavior and make it their calling card. These foot-in-mouth offenders have different root causes. Some No-Filter leaders can't help having verbal diarrhea, because they have low self-awareness and poor social skills. This behavior is perceived as either offensive and rude or offbeat and irrelevant.

1) Offensive and Rude

No-Filter leaders who are offensive and rude often have difficulty empathizing with others. Although some might be described as amiable, warm, and personable, their comments don't show it. They frequently make insensitive comments without realizing it. These No-Filters can't put themselves in others' shoes and don't understand how their words are perceived. They often unintentionally offend or embarrass others. When this is explained to them, they get it, but it's after the damage has already been done. These people make poor leaders and are a public relations nightmare for companies

2) Offbeat and Irrelevant

Some No-Filters don't say anything inappropriate or offensive, but their comments are frequently a little off topic. Many get a reputation for being unusual or quirky because of how they act or what they say in social situations. Because they have trouble gauging others' reactions, they might take conversations in strange directions or contribute through non-sequiturs. When people laugh at their comments or get confused, it's hard for these No-Filter leaders to understand why—or worse, they take it as a compliment.

> " Whenever I watch TV and see those poor starving kids all over the world, I can't help but cry. I mean I'd love to be skinny like that, but not with all those flies and death and stuff. "
> - Mariah Carey

Mariah Carey, singer, can sometimes take things in a strange direction.

Other No-Filter leaders just seem to never stop talking. They aren't good at reading others' reactions or picking up on social cues to understand when people aren't interested in listening. Spending time with this type of person can be exhausting and highly unproductive in the workplace. Even though their comments start off as relevant, they quickly derail, taking meetings with them. People who are focused, productive, and aware of social norms and etiquette have a hard time conversing with these leaders. They want to be polite, so they'll let the No-Filter talk, but it often becomes clear the person has no intention to stop talking anytime soon. It's hard to get a word in edgewise or get the conversation back on track without aggressively interrupting.

Poor Donald Rumsfeld, former U.S. Secretary of Defense, just can't stop talking.

> " Reports that say that something hasn't happened are always interesting to me, because as we know, there are known knowns; there are things we know we know. We also know there are known unknowns; that is to say we know there are some things we do not know. But there are also unknown unknowns – the ones we don't know we don't know.
> - Donald Rumsfeld "

For example, I once worked with a woman who talked on and on in meetings when she was asked to introduce herself. People started to look around the room at others' reactions because it was bizarre and embarrassing. Because of her, the company actually changed its approach to team members' introductions at clients' meetings. Each employee was instructed to say only his or her name, position, and one sentence about his or her involvement on the project. The new rules worked to keep our No-Filter colleague's introduction short and sweet, but it was sad it had to come to that point.

Both offensive and offbeat No-Filters don't just have their foot in their mouth at work. They are also equal opportunity offenders who act in the same clueless way outside the office.

3) The No-Filter by Choice

No-Filter leaders who take pride in their loose lips are another story entirely. Encouraged by the shocked reactions and laughter of their coworkers, they relish being the entertainment in the workplace. They happily assume this role and coworkers often give them a pass for their bad behavior. This encourages No-Filters to up their game, and they continue interrupting with rude or obnoxious comments. Like a child seeking attention any way he can get it, this type of No-Filter thrives on getting a rise out of people.

A friend of mine recently saw this play out at a company party where employees and their families had gathered. A group of people was discussing Myers-Briggs types, which are typically referenced as acronyms. The wife of one of the employees asked what type her husband was. His boss piped up, "That's obvious! He's a S-H-I-T." Even though it got some laughs, the wife flushed deeply; both she and her husband were embarrassed by the joke. It was an awkward moment, especially because the wife wasn't familiar with the leader's brash style. She didn't know how to react. People who choose not to filter their comments make others feel uncomfortable, which isn't productive in the workplace.

Kanye West, singer, likes to draw attention to himself and often embarrasses others in the process.

> **I can't do this show until everybody stands up...**
> **...OK, you're fine. - Kanye West**

After demanding that concertgoers get up and dance, Kanye West recently stopped a show in Sydney, Australia when he saw a couple of fans defy his wishes. "I can't do this show until everybody stands up," he screamed. As those nearest the crowd turned to stare, one of the singled-out audience members waved a prosthetic leg in the air. Both fans were in wheelchairs and physically couldn't stand up. "OK, you're fine," Kanye said.

The Authenticity Argument

No-Filters, who assume their role with a badge of honor, typically take pride in their authenticity. In their eyes, they say what other people are thinking but are afraid to say. They despise the Chameleon and the Manipulator because they are so fake. To No-Filters, truth is king. Authenticity can be admirable, but like all things there is a broad spectrum. A healthy range varies depending on the behavior, but being at the extreme end of any spectrum often causes other issues.

For example, saying exactly what you think one hundred percent of the time is certainly authentic, but likely more authenticity than your coworkers need or want. Most often, our thoughts need a little cleaning up before they enter the world; this makes sure they don't offend or hurt others, create a liability for organizations, ourselves or become counter-productive. That's where the filter comes in. Has your significant other has ever asked you the dreaded question, "Does this make me look fat?" If so, you have already gone through a valuable lesson on the importance of filters and/or authenticity.

Overuse of a filter could hold back so much information that you are perceived as inauthentic, but underuse of a filter could let comments through that are better left unsaid, making a person seem like a real jerk. It is important for people with filter problems to understand this balance between being authentic and being totally insensitive to others. Unless people consider their true nature to be insensitive and hurtful to others, using a filter shouldn't compromise their ability to be authentic.

Career Development

Lack of filtering in the workplace can hinder career development whether the behavior is intentional or unintentional. Regardless of the industry or organization, it's hard to avoid workplace politics. No-Filter leaders may be tolerated and their behavior overlooked at some levels, but it's likely that they will be passed over for a promotion because their behavior is seen as too risky and volatile. Even though they're admired for their candor, they are seen as people who always need supervision when meeting with clients, addressing large employee audiences, or making public statements. As managers advance within an organization, job duties such as these often become an integral part of their role. Instead of gaining more freedom of speech, senior leaders usually experience an even greater filter imposed by company owners, investors, or the board. Such experiences can be frustrating even for leaders who have a healthy filter.

An acquaintance of mine experienced this when his company went through their first Initial Public Offering (IPO). As CEO, he was selected to give the announcement speech, which was first reviewed by the investor relations officer and the company's general counsel. After receiving the edited version of his speech that left out most of the details he wanted to share, he realized he was now operating under a different level of filter. Even though the IPO certainly advanced his career, it didn't come without cost to his freedom of speech. Commenting on the situation, he said, "Soon they'll be telling me I can only talk about the weather."

It is easy to see how people who choose not to use the company filters that are suggested to them would not be successful in a role that requires them to conduct presentations for the company.

Can No-Filters Change Their Ways?

Those who are agreeable to filtering their comments have a better chance at changing than No-Filters who take pride in their behavior. If a No-Filter employee reports to you, the following strategies are effective in helping her gain self-awareness:

The WAIT Game

☐ WAIT is the acronym for Why Am I Talking? If your direct report could benefit from more listening and less talking, tell her to think WAIT before speaking at a meeting. If she doesn't have a good contribution, she should WAIT until she has something valuable to say.

Scripting and Rehearsing

☐ Instead of speaking off the cuff and inserting foot-in-mouth, No-Filters benefit from rehearsing speeches, presentations, and the answers to questions they are likely to be asked. By getting feedback from trusted advisors, they can adjust their approach in a safe dry-run situation, hopefully avoiding issues when they go live.

Discuss Do's and Don'ts

☐ When you manage a No-Filter employee, the rule is better safe than sorry. Before important meetings with clients or coworkers, discuss topics that are hot buttons. Talk specifically about what should or should not be said and explain why. Make sure the direct report takes notes and uses them so you don't have to waste time going over the same information. In addition, you could have the direct report lead the discussion with you, rehearsing it first and incorporating tips you've provided.

Create a Secret Signal

☐ When a No-Filter colleague is venturing into dangerous waters, it's helpful to have a signal that tells that person to stop talking. I worked with a No-Filter colleague for years and whenever he would start to say something inappropriate, I would scratch my nose. It helped him realize when he was about to or already had crossed the line; as time passed, we both noticed I was scratching my nose less and less.

Address Insensitive Comments

☐ When a direct report or a colleague unknowingly says something that offends others, speak up and let that person know. You can say something like, "I know you aren't an insensitive/prejudiced person, but when you said ___, it came across that way." (It might be a difficult conversation to have, but it could help prevent future problems.)

No-Filters can improve, but it will take time and serious effort. Like teenagers, No-Filters eventually grow out of their political mishaps, learning from their mistakes. As a leader, the best you can do is offer guidance and take advantage of teachable moments. It is far better to prepare rather than conduct damage control later.

If you have the opportunity to give advice to a No-Filter, fill your advice with tangible examples. If you work with a No-Filter colleague who thinks he's just being authentic, make sure you clearly explain to him when his remarks were hurtful, embarrassing to others, or have caused organizational chaos.

What if You Have a No-Filter Boss?

If the boss doesn't combine Tyrant or User and Abuser characteristics with No-Filter traits, then you will probably like reporting to him. People typically like reporting to a No-Filter leader, because what they see is what they get; employees find that reassuring. Unfortunately, if you are a direct report, you are not in a great position to coach your No-Filter boss. Trust me, I attempted it once and it did not go well. If your boss knows she needs help and asks for your assistance, it's best to recommend hiring a professional coach, who specializes in workplace communication. It will be worth the investment.

At some point you need to take a step back, realizing there is only so much you can do to help your boss. If you continue to work for this boss, you will need to manage your professional relationship. You may want to create a little distance between yourself and your boss. Guilt by association is common, and you probably don't want your colleagues to think you have the same viewpoints as your No-Filter Leader. If your boss has been speaking on your behalf, you may want to take appropriate opportunities and identify your own opinions about work projects. This should be done with professional respect and without creating more damage for your boss or yourself.

What if *You* Occasionally Have No-Filter?

If any of these situations sound familiar on a personal level, you may be suffering from a lack of filter. Don't despair! You can increase your self-awareness, become more politically savvy and get your career back on the fast track. Try the following tips:

- ☐ Practice the WAIT method at the office and in social situations. Before you speak, evaluate whether your comment adds value to the discussion topic.

- ☐ Treat every piece of information you receive as confidential unless you are told otherwise. This will help you avoid accidentally spreading gossip. This will also help you avoid being the Manipulator's pawn. A skilled Manipulator knows all he has to do to control the rumor mill is to pass information to a No-Filter. Don't be that person.

- ☐ Pay attention to your audience's reaction when you speak. Do they look bored? Annoyed? Do they roll their eyes and smirk at each other when you open your mouth? These are all signs you might need to rein it in and collect your thoughts before sharing them.

- ☐ Ask a trusted colleague or friend to be your eyes and ears and provide you with timely and candid feedback. And don't behave defensively when you get what you asked for! Listen, reflect, and act on it.

In Meetings:

- [ ] Do *not* be the first person to talk.

    - [ ] Don't add to other people's comments, especially in client meetings, unless you have something different or of value to say.

    - [ ] Don't ask more than two questions in a presentation or panel. In fact, try to keep it to one good question.

    - [ ] Ask yourself if your comment is a mere repetition of what somebody else has already said.

    - [ ] If you are going to take a controversial or unusual position, make sure to have your facts and analysis straight.

    - [ ] Speak only for yourself. Do not say, "Mary also supports this point of view." Even if Mary does agree with you, she might not be happy to be put on the spot. Instead, you can say, "You might want to check with Mary on what she thinks about this." That is as far as you want to go to avoid creating drama.

- [ ] If you make an insensitive comment, acknowledge your *faux pas* and apologize on the spot. Rather than saying something that came out wrong just say that what you said wrong or uncalled for, apologize and leave it at that. Acknowledging mistakes and not repeating mistakes will go a long way in establishing credibility.

Summary

There is a reason why mind reading is a terrifying concept; our thoughts usually need a filter before they enter this world. The next time you aren't sure if you should open your mouth, WAIT before you speak, because some things are better left unsaid. The more you exercise this good habit, the more others will see you as a thoughtful colleague who contributes value in the workplace.

CHAPTER SEVEN

THE LANDGRABBER

Even though this may be an unfamiliar term, it's an all-too-familiar offensive behavior—not just in the workplace, but also in life. Chances are you've had a long history of dealing with landgrabbing, whether you recognized it or not. The Landgrabber is the toddler who yells, "Mine, mine, mine," when she sees anything she wants; it's the grandfather who refuses to throw anything away; it's the friend who asks for a portion of your lunch before he takes a bite of his own; and it's the dog who crams two tennis balls in his mouth while pawing at the one you're holding.

Landgrabbers have an insatiable appetite for *stuff* and it doesn't necessarily matter what it is. If they see it as having value to someone, it must be beneficial, and they want it. In their eyes, resources are currency. If these resources aren't worth anything now, they hold onto them for their future trading value. Depending on the situation, you may have viewed your Landgrabbers' experiences as amusing, irritating, or infuriating. Or maybe you didn't notice anything because you were just a pawn in the Landgrabber's game.

In the workplace, landgrabbing causes a wide array of issues. Not only does it make people mad enough to quit, it can compromise productivity, waste money, and create chaos. In this chapter, we will uncover the major ways Landgrabbers try to get their grubby hands on anything valuable, and how to stop them dead in their tracks.

What a Landgrabber Looks Like

Research shows that personality is a key determinant of people's ability or inability to behave in the workplace. Personality assessments capture aspects of personality that predict behavior. The Hogan Development Survey (HDS) assesses the dark side of personality, identifying toxic and nonproductive behaviors that can and do derail careers. The table that follows identifies the three HDS scales that a Landgrabber will typically score high on (7 or greater on a 10-point scale). Landgrabbers are skeptical, mischievous and imaginative. They will go after your budget dollars, office space, work resources and even your employees. They are individuals

The Landgrabber's Leadershit Behaviors	
Three Highest *HDS Scores	How the Landgrabber will behave in the workplace based on *HDS scores
Skeptical	Sensitive to criticism, argumentative, critical of others, defensive, easily angered, suspicious of others' intentions, prone to faultfinding.
Mischievous	Makes intuitive (not data-base) decisions, unwilling to follow others' rules, may not learn from past mistakes, takes risks without reviewing consequences, pushes the limits, ignores commitments, motivated by pleasure.
Imaginative	Different perspectives and ideas, poor influence and persuasion skills, whimsical and eccentric, Potentially creative—but off mark, preoccupied, unconventional, unaware of how their actions affect others.
Examples	Vladimir Putin
*The Hogan Development Survey (HDS) evaluates the dark side of personality, identifying overused strengths and toxic assets that will derail careers if the behaviors are not kept in check.	

who are suspicious of others' intentions and are often unaware of how their behavior affects others.

Understanding the Landgrabbing Mindset

To beat them, you must first understand them. At the core, Landgrabbers are driven by an enormous insecurity. They are nervous about what the future might hold, so they want to be as well-positioned today as possible.

Many children start out as mini-Landgrabbers. They are demanding and selfish; they don't want to share and have trouble empathizing with others. In essence, they need to be socialized. As parents, we work hard to teach our children to put others first. Hopefully, these efforts are rewarded. As children age, they gain emotional maturity and often grow out of their landgrabbing tendencies.

Sometimes landgrabbing behaviors can be the result of experiencing some form of hardship. People who survived the Great Depression have been known for being thrifty years after the economy and their bank accounts recovered. Even as middle class or wealthy adults, many couldn't help wondering if their jobs and money would disappear again and they would have to make do with what they had. As a result, their landgrabbing looks like hoarding; they never throw anything away. It's easier to be sympathetic to Landgrabbers who have experienced hardship than Landgrabbers who haven't.

Some landgrabbing adults are simply immature and insecure; they suffer a deep-seeded fear of being a nobody—a failure. They are afraid of not being successful, not living up to standards, and ultimately, not being respected. They see accumulating resources as a way to gain power, success, security, and respect; so they push through life taking as much as they can. They are primarily money-driven and materialistic; they get pleasure from having more than others and owning things for the sake of owning things. They often think others view resources the same way; this drives them to take-take-take before someone takes something from them. As a young professional, they might get a pass because others will see their behavior as immature, but ten years later that explanation will no longer hold.

The hardcore Landgrabbers may give others the impression that they have a psychological issue. They exhibit anxiety, paranoia, and extreme selfishness, often isolating themselves from society. The television show, *Hoarders,* gives an intimate look inside the homes of some of these troubled individuals. Before the show's hosts can clean up a house, they work with hoarders to try to clean up their mindset. The piles of stuff aren't the real problem; the real problem is the hoarder not being able to let go of any physical objects.

Keep in mind not all Landgrabbers hoard material possessions. In the workplace, the hoarded resources are often intangible, making Landgrabbers harder to identify. The following sections highlight the top resources Landgrabbers typically go after.

Grab Those Employees

You. That's right. If you are an employee, there is probably a Landgrabber who wants *you* as a resource. To protect yourself and coworkers, you need to know why some people want to landgrab employees, and how they get away with it.

John, a marketing manager, approaches you at the water cooler. He tells you about a new important project and he thinks you have a unique skillset that would benefit the project team. He invites you to the meeting to connect with the team and see how you can contribute. Because John's manager is higher up the food chain than you, you're flattered and feel you are gaining credibility around the office. At the meeting, you commit to providing a lot of support, and honestly, you feel pretty good about it. It's great to be needed and appreciated. You leave the office hoping to adjust deadlines for other projects you already told your boss you would meet.

The next day, when you speak with your boss and tell her your involvement in this new project, she gets upset. What about your responsibilities within your own department? If you had time for more work, why didn't you let her know? She tells you she doesn't want you working on this project and to let John know you can't help after all. You are taken aback by her response. You feel like your boss is selfish and that she doesn't care about your career development. You wish you reported to John who clearly values you more than your own boss.

When companies don't have effective Human Resource policies, Landgrabbers feed on the human resources inside the organization.

What just happened here? Simple, you were landgrabbed. John found a way to impress his boss and get more done by tapping into someone else's resources. Instead of asking your boss whether you could help, John, the Landgrabber, bypassed her and talked directly to you. What's more, he presented it like a great opportunity, flattered you, and made you want to participate. If you think that wasn't planned, you're fooling yourself. Of course, John knew your boss wouldn't want you spending a lot of time working on a project for another department. What manager wants that? It isn't that departments should be territorial or uncooperative. However, all departments should prioritize and communicate their projects and goals. This will help everyone determine whether they can take on extra work that doesn't contribute to those priorities or goals. Your boss understands this and has a right to be upset that John tricked you into doing work that supported his agenda. Unfortunately, your boss is the one who comes out of this situation looking bad. Depending on how intent the Landgrabber is on gaining you as a resource and how naïve you are, it could get even more ugly.

Let's say you go back to John and share the news that your boss won't let you work on the new project. John might say something like, "That's terrible that your boss is being territorial. This project would be really great for your career. Hmmm... I might actually have a good solution! How much are you making now? ...That's it? I could give you a 15% increase. Why don't you come work for me?"

It feels like your stars have just aligned. Soon you'll be making more money, working on an important project, and reporting to a manager who cares about your career. And it all fell right into your lap! You transfer departments before your boss knows what hit her. It all happened so fast; you didn't even consider the big picture. How do you think your actions will affect your coworkers' perceptions of your old boss and John? Your actions said it all. You picked the Landgrabber over your old boss; he must be a superior manager.

Believe it or not, this situation happens all the time. When companies don't have effective Human Resource policies, Landgrabbers feed on the human resources inside the organization. Contrary to what you might think, executives and boards tend to love Landgrabbers because they come across as aggressive managers who get things done. They don't ask for resources or permission. They take matters into their own hands and drive outcomes that get noticed. If a situation is called into question, executives typically side with Landgrabbers because they value productivity and self-starters, completely overlooking the organizational dysfunction. If employees were able to help out on a project outside of their department, they must not have had enough to do. If employees decide to leave a department to work for a Landgrabber in another department, they must have been unhappy before; the company is lucky to retain them. When other managers complain about having their people grabbed, they just look like complainers. It's unfair, but true.

Even though executives and boards may not always recognize landgrabbing, it creates chaos. It puts leaders who follow the rules at a disadvantage and creates a culture that values internal competition more than teamwork.

Power in Numbers

You may not have noticed, but there's a price on your head—actually, on everyone's head. Employees represent money in the budget; Landgrabbers take pride in having one more minion. It's like building an army; they brag about how many soldiers they have marching in the corporate line behind them. It doesn't matter whether the employees are brilliant and talented or just warm bodies; Landgrabbers focus on head count. In fact, some landgrabbing leaders will even avoid firing bad employees, because they are afraid they won't get a replacement. Hiring freezes cramp Landgrabbers' style. If bringing in new talent isn't an option, Landgrabbers hold onto their direct reports even tighter.

How to Protect Yourself When Leaders Get Grabby

Communicate openly with direct reports: Make sure your team understands the organizational structure and how individual departments are responsible for their own goals and budgets. Explain how interdepartmental projects work and how all managers must approve them. This actually protects employees from taking on additional or unnecessary work.

Log your hours and charge for your time: When someone from another department needs help, try to determine if it supports the company overall or if it seems that it is most beneficial to the requester. Research departments are especially vulnerable to one-off requests from client-facing staff, who want to look good in front of their customers. Companies can't be productive when individual departments are stuck putting in a lot of work that only helps a few people.

With that type of request, advise your employees to log their hours. If work takes under two hours or a reasonable timeframe, instruct your employees to help them. If it takes too much time, inform the requester that he will have to pay for the labor from his department's budget. It's miraculous how this policy will cut back on urgent interdepartmental requests.

Ask how the credit will be split: Landgrabbers butter people up to get as much help as they can. However, when it comes to taking credit for the outcomes, they like to stand alone. When you're dealing with a known Landgrabber, tell them upfront that you want credit for helping and get an agreement in writing. Say you will document the time spent and the aspects you managed and the senior leadership will know it was a combined effort. If this sounds pushy, that's because it is. Landgrabbers are shameless, so you have to be firm and direct to stand up to them.

Strength in Human Resources: A strong Human Resources department can prevent employee landgrabbing. Staff shouldn't be allowed to make job offers directly to existing employees in other departments without going through a process. Any staffing changes should be discussed with Human Resources and with both managers. Executives should take violations of this policy seriously and hold the violators accountable.

Grab Those Budgets

Getting a bigger piece of the pie is a landgrabbing leader's top priority. More money in the budget means more projects, more people, and most of all, more power.

When planning the upcoming year's budget, most Landgrabbers will ask for more money than they need. This allows room to expand. Another popular strategy is to propose an overly optimistic number of projects, which means extra money to fund the projects. It's negotiation: people ask for more than they think they'll actually get. This ensures that if projects get cut, the money they get is still above the minimum.

During the fiscal year, Landgrabbers will try to dip into other departments' budgets. They are surprisingly aware of how other teams spend their money and who has extra for the taking.

I was in a meeting once where Jack, a seasoned Landgrabber, proposed a new idea to the CEO. The CEO loved it, but he questioned where the company would find the money. Jack didn't miss a beat. "It could come out of Tom's budget," he said. "Correct me if I'm wrong, but Tom hasn't used a good chunk of his budget and doesn't have it allocated to specific projects." Tom was obviously not expecting this inquiry, and he couldn't provide a quick enough reason why he needed to keep the money. At Jack's suggestion, the CEO approved the idea and funded it from Tom's budget. Jack became so notorious for pulling this kind of maneuver that his peers were wary. He worked remotely and when he would come to the office, someone would joke, "Jack is here! Hide your wallets!"

Another sneaky thing Landgrabbers do is misrepresent expenses by charging them to different budgets. By the time an accounting supervisor notices the error, it's already done and on the books.

Organizational Design

Some organizational structures make landgrabbing much harder than others. Centralized organizations, where one chief executive manages each department across all locations, typically do a better job of safeguarding against landgrabbing. Each chief executive meets with their unit managers in each location to create a budget, and the budget is firm for the year. If a unit needs more resources, they have to request it, make a case for it, and identify the return on investment. If approved, the additional money is recorded on the unit's profit and loss statement. In other words, the unit is charged for extra resources. This holds Landgrabbers accountable for their spending. Colleagues are no longer able to dip into each others' budgets, because the executive controls the money.

Centralizing departments allows for better checks and balances, improving the way companies spend money. This model works well for both large and small companies. Smaller organizations simply have a regimented process where employees must get formal approval for changes to their budgets.

How to Protect Your Budget

Plan: It is risky to over budget. You should have a clear plan in place that allocates your budget dollars to specific projects and expenditures. Otherwise it may look like you don't need the money. If you have Landgrabbers in your organization, they will be looking to use anything that looks like excess. Don't put money in the general expense category because it looks like extra dollars to Landgrabbers and maybe even your boss.

Customers and Accounts

Landgrabbers exercise their evil powers with clients as well. Client-facing roles can become internally competitive when commissions and egos are on the line. After all, there's no better way to look good than to bring in revenue and build a loyal customer base. However, problems arise when employees landgrab from each other rather than trying to grab externally at new market share. Depending on an organization's policy for managing accounts, Landgrabbers can easily take over client relationships even though they are already being well-managed by their colleagues.

For example, the account manager will bring team members to a client's meeting to offer more support and show that the company is dedicating enough resources to their account. If one of these resources is a Landgrabber, she may quickly take control of the meeting. She may assert herself by volunteering to take notes on the whiteboard or flip chart; this is sometimes called *holding the marker*. This indicates a position of authority to clients and heightens the amount of face time. As questions arise, the Landgrabber will quickly volunteer to follow up with the client. Before you know it, the account manager can say goodbye to that client because the Landgrabber has taken over.

Geographical territories are another risky resource when Landgrabbers are around because they love to expand. If territories are divided by geographical location, Landgrabbers will suggest changing the boundaries so they can have more states or countries. They might even argue that it would be doing a favor for another sales representative, because it would take some responsibility off of his or her plate. Landgrabbers love to seem altruistic. If a territory opens, the Landgrabber likes to swoop in and take over immediately. Even though executives might see this as being helpful, it can actually be detrimental to the sales team and company overall. Other sales staff who are hardworking and good at their jobs can get screwed by this greedy colleague, someone who might not actually be able to manage that many accounts anyway. When the Landgrabber has too much on his plate, customer service starts to suffer and all territories he manages are at risk.

> **Most Landgrabbers don't take things because they think they should be the rightful owner; they take them because they can.**

How to Protect Customers and Accounts

Establish clear policies: Put policies in place so that everyone knows what happens when a territory becomes available. You want to avoid a free-for-all.

I've actually seen a CEO put a territory up for grabs with the sales team; it was set-up as a means for leadership self-selection. Of course, sharp elbowing and chaos ensued. Multiple Landgrabbers tore each other apart vying for the new territory and it was ugly. Less greedy sales representatives, who would have done a good job, didn't step up because they didn't want to get involved in workplace conflict. Clients were uncomfortable because the sales team spent more time competing amongst themselves than providing customer service and support. In the end, the whole sales team was bitter and the Landgrabber was overextended. Don't let this happen at your organization.

Don't allow hostile takeovers: Employees should be told that they can't simply swoop in and become the new point person for an existing client relationship. Accounts should only be transitioned for good reasons with prior planning and a manager's approval. It would be helpful if the company made this part of their sales process.

Summary

Landgrabbing is one of the most common forms of leadershit. In some ways, Landgrabbers are similar to Users and Abusers, but without the sense of entitlement. Most Landgrabbers don't take things because they think they should be the rightful owner; they take them because they can. Your job is to let them know it's not okay to take-take-take. By following the measures in this chapter, you will be well-positioned to stand your ground. Undoubtedly, your organization will be better off when people aren't allowed to behave this way.

CHAPTER EIGHT

THE UNACCOUNTABLE

Tim was the Human Resources Director at a company that makes packaged snacks. Although he was very experienced with human resources policies and procedures, his office always looked as though a small tornado had recently touched down. Unfortunately for everyone involved, many of the documents he managed were paper, rather than electronic. They included original signatures and confidential information.

These documents were one-of-a-kind and/or potentially risky if they fell into the wrong hands. Tim's administrator, Taneka, typically received these documents and submitted them to Tim for approval and processing. Quite often employees would call Taneka and ask why their raise hadn't appeared on their last paycheck, or why their new-hire paperwork was taking so long to process. Taneka would then relay these questions to Tim, who would claim to have zero knowledge of the paperwork. Taneka knew that she had put the documents on Tim's desk or handed them to him directly. However, Tim just never seemed to have any recollection of having received or seen the documents. Suddenly and mysteriously the paperwork was nowhere to be found.

This pattern of missing paperwork became extremely problematic; it created extra administrative work and made the company look terribly disorganized. So Taneka had to be transparent with employees. She had to ask employees to fill out new hire paperwork a second time. Many of them got upset and worried about identity theft because documents with their social security numbers were missing.

After this happened numerous times, Taneka felt like she was going crazy. Was it possible that Tim was frequently misplacing documents and avoiding accountability? To be sure, Taneka started sending follow-up emails to Tim each time she gave him hardcopy documents. The follow-up emails proved that Tim was indeed losing or misplacing documents. From then on, when Tim lost documents, which he continued to do, he had to admit to it.

What an Unaccountable Looks Like

Research shows that personality is a key determinant of people's ability or inability to behave in the workplace. Personality assessments capture aspects of personality that predict behavior. The Hogan Development Survey (HDS) assesses the dark side of personality, identifying toxic and

The Unaccountable's Leadershit Behaviors	
Three Highest *HDS Scores	How the Unaccountable will behave in the workplace based on *HDS scores
Cautious	Slow to make decisions, resistant to change, reluctant to take chances, motivated not to fail, unassertive, conservative, perceived as holding others back.
Leisurely	Seemingly cooperative, unwilling to confront others, doesn't understand sense of urgency, passive resistance, works on own timetable, hard to coach, stubborn, procrastinates when performing uninteresting work.
Dutiful	Compliant, reluctant decision-maker, unwilling to challenge status quo, conforming, strong desire to please others, doesn't stand up for subordinates
Examples	Tony Hayward (BP oil spill), Gregg Steinhafel (Target data breach)
*The Hogan Development Survey (HDS) evaluates the dark side of personality, identifying overused strengths and toxic assets that will derail careers if the behaviors are not kept in check.	

nonproductive behaviors that can and do derail careers. The table that follows identifies the three HDS scales that an Unaccountable will typically score high on (7 or greater on a 10-point scale). Unaccountable leaders do not take responsibility for their actions and avoid committing to goals or other measureable results. They are seen as leisurely, mischievous, and cautious. They like to work according to their own rules and timetables and are often not very loyal to their teams.

Even though the Unaccountable leader doesn't attack colleagues directly, his behavior can deeply damage company culture and productivity, creating a negative effect on those around him. Unaccountable behavior is the failure to admit fault, take responsibility, or acknowledge that taking different actions would have produced better results. Sometimes it's crystal clear when people are being unaccountable, but other times it's harder to recognize, especially when we want to give people the benefit of the doubt.

Maybe foreseeing that disaster truly wasn't possible.

Maybe it wasn't in his power to fix.

Maybe she encountered too many obstacles to reach the goal.

Maybe, but maybe not.

Unaccountable leaders have a knack for avoiding responsibility when something goes wrong. They make us question whether they are victims or innocent bystanders rather than the source of the problem. And they often get away with it, at least in isolated incidents. After all, many of us want to see the best in others and we know that things don't always go perfectly. Looking for someone to blame in every situation is petty and pointless. Unaccountables often receive our sympathy, until we start seeing a pattern in behavior and wonder if we're being hoodwinked. When the same person fails to deliver over and over again, it raises eyebrows. Either that person is extremely unlucky to keep encountering unfortunate situations, or he is the source of the problem and can't admit it.

In the workplace, failing to reach goals not only warrants scrutiny, it can be grounds for dismissal. Unaccountables are highly aware of this. They work hard to avoid taking on responsibility for anything that could potentially go wrong. In fact, many navigate their entire career paths avoiding situations in which they could be held accountable.

Unaccountables are the ultimate can't-do people.

Here are some ways to spot an Unaccountable at your company:

- ☐ Extreme aversion to risk: He would rather hide in the face of opportunity than take a chance on anything that isn't one hundred percent certain to pan out.

- ☐ Avoids documenting goals: Rather than rise to a challenge, the Unaccountable sees outcomes as an opportunity to fail. If goals cannot be avoided, he will set them as low as possible.

- ☐ Shares responsibility instead of owning it: When given responsibility, he will name coworkers to share in delivering those results. If anything goes wrong, it'll be easier to avoid accountability later.

- ☐ Focuses on processes over outcomes: When presenting work in progress, he hones in on processes and activities as opposed to results.

- ☐ Is great at saying no: When faced with new projects or requests, the Unaccountable exerts considerable effort in explaining why something can't be done. In fact, the Unaccountable is known to spend more effort avoiding the work than it would take to actually do the work.

Unaccountables are the ultimate can't-do people.

Organizational Culture and Harboring Unaccountables

Depending on culture and expectations, some companies have very few Unaccountables whereas others are swimming with them. Unaccountables favor bureaucratic environments because red tape limits productivity so often that people are used to not getting anything done. Unaccountables also hide well in larger organizations or situations where responsibilities are diluted and ambiguous. They love elusive positions where colleagues don't really understand what they do.

If you've seen the movie *Office Space*, you may remember when outside consultants are brought in to assess the value of various positions so they can help management decide whom to lay off. Some employees are terrified because senior management will finally realize they serve no purpose and have been doing virtually nothing for years. It's a satire of corporate culture that portrays perfectly what unaccountability looks like.

Some people are happy to coast along, going through the motions of work without ever producing meaningful outcomes. No one gives them specific or measurable goals and they don't publicly set any for themselves. Unaccountables consider this an ideal working environment because their top priority is to avoid clear-cut situations where they are expected to deliver. They fear failure. They don't see challenges as exciting or interesting, they see them as stressful and scary. So they avoid responsibility like the plague.

Some Typical Unaccountable Statements

- "This decision is above my pay grade."

- "It's not part of my responsibilities."

- "I will document all of the issues associated with approving this project."

- "If Lisa had delivered her part, I would have been able to deliver better results."

- "Let me explain the process and all the activities performed so far..."

If the organizational culture allows these statements to be okay, chances are, Unaccountables will get cozy and choose to stay. Their numbers will only grow over time as others see unaccountable behavior as acceptable and decide to follow suit because it's easier. When accountability isn't valued, why work hard to reach goals when it doesn't really matter?

On the other hand, unaccountable behavior is unacceptable and virtually unheard of in some organizational cultures. In these working environments, the above comments would raise red flags. For example, the Unaccountable is a bad fit for small companies, start-ups, and fast-growing, nimble companies that require performance and results. Unaccountables also struggle in cultures that value employees' ability to create customized solutions, because proactively trying new approaches is not their forte. Most sales roles are also a terrible fit, because performance goals are typically number-oriented and specific and performance is competitive. Unaccountables tend to sense this and many avoid all positions within the realm of sales.

Are Unaccountables Bad People?

After all of this negative talk about Unaccountables, you probably have a picture in your head of someone who is an incompetent and utterly worthless employee. You probably question this person's attitude and disposition in life, aligning his complacency with being a leech on society.

Well, you might be surprised to know that many Unaccountables are perfectly competent and even highly intelligent people. In fact, Unaccountables are often affable, likeable people both in and out of the workplace. I've met a few from Ivy League schools who were actually considered rock star recruiting catches.

One such woman named Alice came highly recommended and apparently experienced great success in her previous position. But when she started a new role at a new company, she struggled, because the new role came with specific metrics that held her accountable for success. This made Alice incredibly uncomfortable. In her past positions, there was never a big chance to fail because there weren't concrete goals. Although Alice's boss and her colleagues had faith in her ability to do well, Alice had trouble believing in herself. The stress made her feel even more insecure and she couldn't take the pressure. She ended up leaving the job for another position that had less specific expectations.

Many Unaccountables are crippled by self-doubt.

This example shows another side to the Unaccountable— the person who is driven to do well, but is crippled by self-doubt. More often than not, this is how Unaccountables feel. Unaccountables aren't bad people and they aren't always bad employees. Many simply doubt their abilities and are afraid to put their performance on the line.

While fear is often the underlying motivational factor for Unaccountables, other people don't usually recognize that. Instead, they see people who avoid challenges and responsibilities. Unaccountables behave in certain ways that tend to set people off. Why? It comes down to the fairness principle. Most working professionals are constantly on the hook for delivering concrete results. They work their asses off to reach their goals even when it seems impossible. These people aren't immune to stress, but they manage it and get the job done. It's easy to see how people who are required to deliver specific results might think it's a little unfair that others don't have to abide by the same standards. Although certain roles naturally come with more specific goals than others, accountable employees could easily start to resent Unaccountables for appearing to having it easy or seeming entitled.

In some cases, Unaccountables may seem to be enjoying the good life. However, much of the time they're just as stressed as the rest of us even though it may seem like they have less to worry about. Unaccountables may annoy us, but they aren't the worst leadershit offenders.

What to do if Your Coworker or Boss is an Unaccountable

☐ In meetings, always ask for clarification on who is responsible for what. Make sure someone sends out the meeting notes to everyone.

☐ If possible, avoid accepting a co-chair, co-leadership, or co-working position with this individual. This will save you a lot of time and effort having to manage things on your own while sharing the credit. If you are not in a position to decline the job sharing, make it clear who is accountable for what. Share your meeting minutes with the extended team. It is wise to assign a teammate to review the status of the action items at the beginning of every working session.

☐ Watch out for the Unaccountable delegating too much to others.

  o Many bosses will assign as much as they can to direct reports so they aren't fully responsible if something goes wrong. If your boss is an Unaccountable, you need to be careful; he or she will not hesitate to blame you when a problem arises. Make sure to get your responsibilities in writing as well as verbally. This clarifies your work on the project and what part your boss will do. If you are blamed for something that wasn't on your task list, you will have a record of this. Most bosses delegate, but you shouldn't have to be responsible for the entire project, especially if the boss volunteered to do some of the work.

  o On the flip side, if things go right, your boss is likely to take credit for your accomplishments. If you sense this coming, you can proactively strike up conversation with your boss and mention how happy you are to be fully leading XYZ project. Then mention to your boss that you hope that he has told his boss how hard both of you are working on this project. If your boss always takes credit for your work and talking with him about it doesn't change anything, you might need to visit with your Human Resource professionals for advice.

How to Make Accountability a Top Priority at Your Organization

One simple solution is to bake accountability into the performance review. Author, speaker, and leadership consultant Kevin Sheridan did this at his former consulting company, HR Solutions. Accountability has always been a strong personal value of Sheridan's and in founding HR Solutions; he wanted to make sure his employees held the same values. That's why he built the company's performance review to weigh accountability higher than other performance metrics. In fact, accountability counted three times more than the other metrics. Sheridan cared about the other metrics assessed on employees' reviews, but his non-negotiable has always been accountability.

"Nobody is perfect," Sheridan says. "But when an employee makes mistakes, it's important that he or she is transparent and accountable so that issues can be fixed immediately."

All HR Solutions employees became aware of how important accountability was when they learned about performance reviews during new-hire orientation. As a result, when HR Solutions employees made mistakes, they proactively informed their managers. There was honor in being forthright about imperfections rather than trying to hide them.

Sheridan sold HR Solutions a few years ago, but he continues to consult with organizations independently on how to foster an engaged, productive culture. He strongly believes that you can't improve what you don't measure. If accountability needs a boost at your organization, Sheridan highly recommends adding it as a metric in performance reviews.

What to do if You See the Unaccountable in You?

- ☐ If your unaccountability stems from a fear of having less than perfect results, remind yourself that no one is perfect. People try their best and that's all anyone can expect from them. If things don't go as well as planned, don't consider it a failure and hide under a rock. If you're trying your best to be productive, to challenge yourself, and to make the company a better place, you should be confident and proud. Know that people will respect you for having tried and taken responsibility for the outcome.

- ☐ Take note of how often you find yourself explaining to colleagues why something won't be easy to do or shouldn't be done. Try thinking about those projects as personal challenges rather than risks. If you track how long it takes you to complete some of those tasks you dread, you may realize they weren't nearly as difficult as you thought. Try saying yes to new projects, setting goals for yourself, and recording your outcomes. You may be surprised at how often you succeed.

Summary

Being accountable is highly regarded because it isn't always easy. It takes courage to face challenges that you might fail at and own up to them when you should have done something differently. Even though accountability can be scary, it's smart to think of it as a win-win: you succeed and take pride in your accomplishment, or you fall short but gain respect by taking responsibility. Keep this in mind, because being unaccountable is a loser's strategy.

CHAPTER NINE

THE INAUTHENTIC

An elusive but honorable quality, authenticity often favorably tips the likeability and followership scales for leaders. Although we can't always put our finger on what authenticity looks like, it's what we try to sniff out in politicians, celebrities, salespeople, and friends. Authenticity puts us at ease because we feel like we understand other peoples' choices and actions and we can relate to them on a personal level.

Authenticity is why people love actress Jennifer Lawrence and why they loved her even more when she fell down at the Oscars in 2013 and again at the Oscars in 2014. She's not great at walking in heels and that makes her a real person, not a perfect celebrity. This has contributed to her popularity. It is easy to see why so many people perceive her to be more authentic than other celebrities. (It isn't just because she falls down a lot or many more famous people would be well liked.) It seems like people-pleasing is not a top priority for her—there is something genuine about Jennifer. Her awards acceptance speeches sound like she's talking from her heart to family and close friends; they do not sound like she is trying to impress the entire world. When she accepted the Golden Globe for *Silver Linings Playbook* in 2013, she thanked her brothers for being mean to her, but also for being nice and supportive. It sounded like genuine sibling gratitude, rather than a speech that was cleaned up by a public relations team. Because Jennifer does not try to impress us, we are, in fact, impressed. Jennifer's behavior represents authenticity, but what should we expect from someone who is inauthentic?

What an Inauthentic Leader Looks Like

Research shows that personality is a key determinant of people's ability or inability to behave in the workplace. Personality assessments capture aspects of personality that predict behavior. The Hogan Development Survey (HDS) assesses the dark side of personality, identifying toxic and nonproductive behaviors that can and do derail careers. The table that follows identifies the three HDS scales that an Inauthentic leader will typically score high on (7 or greater on a 10-point scale). They are seen as bold, skeptical, and colorful. At the same time, Inauthentics are self-promoting, demanding, and overbearing with little to no team loyalty.

The Inauthentic's Leadershit Behaviors	
Three Highest *HDS Scores	How the Inauthentic will behave in the workplace based on *HDS scores
Bold	Resistant to feedback, overestimates talents and accomplishments, doesn't seek different opinions, demanding and overbearing, blames mistakes on others, self-promoting, strong sense of entitlement, no team loyalty.
Skeptical	Sensitive to criticism, argumentative, critical, defensive, easily angered, suspicious of others' intentions, prone to fault finding.
Colorful	Self-promoting, attention seeking, poor listening skills, easily distracted, manages by crisis, problems with organization, lacks follow-though
Examples	Mitt Romney
*The Hogan Development Survey (HDS) evaluates the dark side of personality, identifying overused strengths and toxic assets that will derail careers if the behaviors are not kept in check.	

Indeed there are many qualities to like or dislike in a person, but most people have a deep-seeded natural dislike for those who seem fake. Inauthentic people tend to rub us the wrong way and make us suspicious of their real agenda, intentions, and motives. We wonder what they are hiding and we are wary of trusting them.

Considering our inherent distaste for fake behavior, it is natural that we are drawn toward behavior that appears real and trustworthy. We look for this especially in leaders. Whether it's a political leader, CEO, company owner, manager, coach, or volunteer coordinator, authenticity inspires us to follow people and support their missions.

Our appreciation for realness holds true even when leaders make mistakes. Even though people may or may not have agreed with Bill Clinton's political viewpoints, most thought he seemed genuine. In 1998, during his personal scandal and impeachment trial, his approval rating actually hit its highest point at 73 percent. This statistic is curious given that Clinton had just been accused of cheating and lying. It's safe to say that most Americans don't condone that type of behavior, but something about his imperfections made him relatable and authentic, and thus likeable.

The Four Components of Authenticity

Being authentic is the alignment of four things:

- Values: What is truly important to you; what really matters and is non-negotiable.

- Promises: What you promise to do.

- Intentions: What you truly intend to do, whether you promised it or not.

- Actions: At the end of the day, what you actually do.

In a perfect world, being an authentic leader would be easy. Just be yourself, right? However, the business environment is complex and there are often numerous factors that impact behavior and decisions.

For example, let's say that one of your non-negotiable principles is that people should only be rewarded and promoted at work on a merit basis. So you have an employee who is a star and you believe she should be promoted. In fact, you are so confident that you promise her you will do everything in your power to get her promoted, which you truly intend to do. Unfortunately, at the performance review meeting, you realize there are fewer promotion slots than you had assumed and far more politics around selecting candidates. Realizing the political discussions involved, you foresee a potentially negative outcome for yourself, personally, if you stand your ground and push to have your employee promoted over other powerful executives' candidates. At some point, you finally give in so as not to damage your relationships with the executives, your career or your employee's career.

Even though you agreed to the promotions for others because you felt backed into a corner, how do you think your rock star employee will feel? You had assured her she would be promoted. You sounded like you had the power to help her, but then you didn't pull through in the end. She will probably feel deceived or even betrayed and her perception of your authenticity will most certainly take a hit.

This type of situation may sound familiar because it is so common. Employees don't typically see all of the dynamics that go on behind the scenes when it comes to promotions. Instead of understanding that managers don't always get their way, employees tend to think less of their managers. They assume their managers never really had the intention of following through with their promises.

This is the perfect example of why it isn't always easy to be perceived as authentic. In the workplace, leaders can't always do whatever they want even if they're at the top of the corporate ladder. Their values, promises, and intentions can be perfectly aligned, but they encounter a roadblock that stops forward action. What makes matters worse is that exposing the roadblock can involve blaming a colleague, which is something smart leaders will avoid. Even though their heart is in the right place, well-intentioned leaders can sometimes look fake or even scheming and deceitful if a roadblock interferes with their promises or intentions.

Sometimes a lack of foresight and planning can be the root cause of a reputation for being inauthentic. However, inauthentic leadershit comes in many shapes and sizes. Perhaps some of the following stories will sound familiar to you.

The Good News Bearer

Being authentic should be easy—just stay true to yourself and what you believe in and act accordingly. In some situations, it is that easy. Unfortunately, authenticity can be complicated for people who have a lot riding on what others think of them. Leaders who have a lot to lose from a negative image can get caught up in pleasing people, which causes discrepancies between personal values, promises, intentions, and actions. When these four elements aren't aligned, leaders become inauthentic. They suffer, their teams suffer, and at times, the entire organization suffers. Teams lose trust when they don't understand their leaders' principles or what they stand for and the leader becomes unpredictable. This uncertainty makes employees uncomfortable, especially when it comes to something as important as their careers.

These leaders are viewed as inauthentic because they say whatever people want to hear with no intention of following through. Afraid of damaging their own likeability, these leaders get others to take the lead and have the difficult conversations and execute the dirty work.

Meet Nancy, a managing director who fits this leadershit profile. Dee, a senior manager, worked for Nancy. Dee had been involved in the tough decision whether to make the week between Christmas and New Year's Day a paid holiday, giving the staff the week off. Dee's management team weighed the options and was almost unanimously in favor of the idea. The exception was Nancy, who was adamantly opposed; she didn't want to be responsible for lost productivity or have to justify the decision to the board, because she was worried about her personal image. In the end, Dee and her team overpowered Nancy and gave the staff the week off.

Immediately after the decision had been made, Nancy nominated herself to announce the good news. Her selfish behavior and desire to take credit for a decision she didn't support did not go unnoticed by the other executives. Nancy's inauthentic behavior was the misalignment of her values, true intentions, and actions. By trying to win favor with the staff overall, she damaged her credibility with the senior team.

Months later, the same company had some bad news to share with employees. Dee and the senior team came together to discuss a communication plan for sharing this news with staff. Someone suggested that as the leader of the company, it should come from Nancy, the managing director. However, because she likely remembered how good it felt to share the great holiday news, Nancy said, "No, I am the *good* news bearer. I don't share bad news." Another executive spoke up and said, "Leaders who only give good news when there is bad news to be given are seen as fake."

It took guts to criticize Nancy's decision, but the executive was right. It didn't take long for people to see her true colors. It reminds me of the saying, "Fool me once, shame on you. Fool me twice, shame on me." It wasn't smart for Nancy to make communication decisions based on how she thought they would affect her popularity. That is the essence of inauthentic leadershit. What's most interesting is how quickly Nancy lost rapport with the senior team. When people mask their beliefs so easily to please others, it is fake.

What Can We Learn From This Story?

Being a yes-man or yes-woman may gain you favor for a while, but the reality is that you can't always make decisions that will please everyone. At some point, all leaders are faced with the choice of remaining true to their values and making a decision that won't be popular, or compromising their values to please others. When faced with this type of dilemma, leaders should ask themselves a few questions:

At some point, all leaders are faced with the choice of remaining true to their values and making a decision that won't be popular, or compromising their values to please others.

1. If it is so easy for me to take a position that goes against my stated principles, are the principles I articulate really the ones I believe? Or are they just the principles I think respectful leaders should uphold?

   ☐ Make sure you're honest with yourself and stand by principles you truly believe.

2. If I am true to my values and principles, what are the negative consequences of not behaving, and making decisions according to them?

   ☐ Think about the consequences for yourself, your team, and the organization. It may very well be that there are immediate positive consequences for you personally, such as remaining on the good side of a couple of powerful people or avoiding a nasty confrontation. However, you need to think about the broad, long-term implications of the misalignment between your stated principles and your actions.

3. Am I willing to stand up for my values, even when it isn't easy or when it will hurt my short term personal goals?

- ☐ Staying true to your values and principles could cause you to take positions that aren't always popular. You might not earn a spot in the CEO's inner circle of friends or you might lose your spot simply because you challenge your superiors' ideas. In the case of our promotion situation at the beginning of this chapter, an unwavering authentic leader would have confronted her peers and superiors by asking what the promotion criteria were and why her employee was not receiving her deserved promotion. She might even have gone a step further, questioning the values and practices of the company or openly saying that she didn't support a no-promotion decision for her employee. Would that behavior have damaged her career? Quite possibly, but it's a risk that has to be taken if authenticity is a top priority.

Struggling to Walk-the-Walk

Sometimes leaders make promises they intend to keep, but have a difficult time keeping them in the moment of truth. Even though their initial intentions were good, failing to deliver on them can damage perceptions of authenticity.

Meet Jerry, a CEO, who wanted to build a culture of openness in the organization where employees of all levels could communicate casually and frequently. Jerry truly believed this would improve productivity and engagement and felt fully committed to supporting this plan.

That was before a bunch of younger employees attempted friending him on Facebook: they had taken him seriously when he preached open communication through the ranks. Now he was faced with a difficult decision—accept their friend requests, tearing down the thin veil of privacy between his professional and personal life or ignore the employees' requests and risk coming across as inauthentic. Jerry was torn.

When he confided in a close colleague about the situation, she told him that if he wanted to be authentic that he should accept the friend requests. Jerry had claimed that he backed up his words with actions so he shouldn't go against his claim. He shared his intentions of being open with the staff and now he had to follow through with actions. Jerry's colleague asked him what was the worst that could come of being Facebook friends with employees. She suggested that if they communicated with him through the site, he could always reply through company email. Having staff relationships through social media was outside of Jerry's comfort zone, but it didn't necessarily have to be negative or all-inclusive.

Jerry considered this advice and decided to accept the friend requests. As it turns out, the younger employees didn't message him or write on his wall; they just wanted to be Facebook friends or, perhaps, test his courage or intention of building an open and collegial culture. Jerry had every intention of building open communication and by aligning his actions with this intention he proved his authenticity. His efforts to build an open company culture paid off through staff loyalty and productivity.

What Can We Learn From This Story?

As a leader, it's important to do some soul searching and know what you want to support before you start spreading the word to others. Think about potential long-term outcomes, both good and bad. Think through the situation and determine how you feel about it. Predicting possible outcomes will help you better assess whether you're supporting the right decisions that align with your values in the present. If you're having trouble getting on board with an idea today, your values or beliefs aren't supported. In this case, you are likely to flip-flop your thinking later, hurting your credibility more than if you hadn't made the initial statement in the first place.

Being on the Receiving End of Inauthenticity

Reporting to an Inauthentic person is a tricky situation. If you find yourself in this position, you must first determine what kind of inauthenticity you are dealing with—intentional or unintentional. Is your leader being deliberately inauthentic by making false promises or having misaligned intentions? Or is your leader unintentionally failing to follow through with the appropriate actions to back up his values, promises, and intentions? This is an incredibly important distinction and should guide how you handle the situation.

Unfortunately, fake people tend to hate being called out. Go figure! If you approach a deliberately inauthentic person and point out how his values, promises, intentions, and actions are misaligned, he probably won't respond positively. You might have thought you were already in a bad predicament, but this confrontation could take it to another level. When it comes to dealing with this type of individual, you can't do much. Because of the subjective nature of authenticity, bad leaders easily make excuses to justify their behavior, saying decisions were out of their hands. They are used to playing games and most are pretty talented at it. If you report to a person like this, it will be difficult to ever fully trust him. You need to think about how your current position and employer fit into your long-term career goals. It may be in your best interest to remove yourself from a toxic situation.

On the flip side, if you think your leader is unknowingly and unintentionally inauthentic, you can take steps to improve the situation.

If your leader is failing to deliver on promises, you could discuss specific examples of when this behavior occurred and it has subsequently eroded his authenticity. For example, maybe she shared plans for a positive new initiative, but then never implemented the plans. There could be any number of reasons—she hit a roadblock, she got busy and forgot. The problem might not be bad intentions. It could be poor planning and over-promising. Talk to your boss. Tell her how much you and your colleagues were looking forward to the new initiative and how disappointed you are that it didn't happen. Start with a position of empathy. Tell her you know she meant well, but that when things don't happen, it makes people question whether she meant what she promised. This will help reinforce that her team is listening to her and that they do notice when she drops the ball. Keep in mind that this approach works best when you have numerous examples and a boss who is open to feedback.

If you're working with a leader whose personality comes across as fake, there are typically a few root causes. Sometimes people give an inauthentic vibe when they try too hard to say the right thing. They are probably overly scripted: they think hard about what they're going to say or what they definitely are not going to say before they speak. Sometimes scripting can work well and ensures people don't regret what comes out of their mouths, but other times it can come across as forced or mechanical. Think about how politicians answer questions; you can almost see them reading the script they rehearsed, searching for the response to the question, or racking their brains for an answer that loosely relates to the question. When answering questions requires that much advanced planning, people naturally wonder what the speaker is trying to hide. The same holds true with overly scripted business leaders, but sometimes it's because they simply aren't comfortable with speaking in front of large groups, or having a position of authority. To deal with their nerves they over-prepare, which can send up a red flag. So it's possible that your seemingly inauthentic leader isn't that comfortable in his own skin. When this type of leader gets more experience and positive reinforcement from colleagues, his confidence rises and he will typically give off a stronger aura of authenticity.

Other leaders come across as inauthentic because they try so hard to emulate someone they look up to. I once worked with a man who admired his boss so much that he slowly transformed into his Mini-Me. He adopted his boss' lingo and habits, his style of clothes, and ultimately, bought the same car—model and color. He had no idea how his behavior looked to colleagues and that they were making fun of him behind his back. This guy was going through a transformation process based on who he thought was cool—another person at his company. When someone finally told him, he was horrified and embarrassed. He felt like he was being his authentic self, but didn't know how his behavior was being perceived.

Summary

The lesson here is that coming across as authentic is harder than it seems. In fact, this is one of the trickiest leadershit profiles to concretely define, as well as improve upon, because it can be so subjective. A lot of people are trying their best to be themselves, but some are more successful than others. Many leaders simply need a little coaching along the way or more time to feel more comfortable in their own skin. You should know that as far as leadershit goes, Inauthentics may cause you to put your guard up, but they often have their hearts in the right place.

On the other hand, some Inauthentics are beyond help, especially when they exhibit traits from other leadershit profiles, such as the Manipulator or the User and Abuser. When it comes to those individuals, it might be in your best interest to stay as far away from them as possible.

CHAPTER TEN

THE POOR COMMUNICATOR- A BETTER LEADER WITH MOUTH SHUT

The 60-minute presentation is over. The team applauds and leaves the room. And yet the same questions linger in everyone's minds: What did he really say? What does he want us to do? Am I supposed to go right or left?

Unclear communication affects teams of all sizes, shapes and tenures, hindering productivity and effectiveness. Unfortunately, it can be a hard problem to identify, because people aren't always quick to speak up and let others know that they are confused. Instead, many second-guess whether it's their own fault for not understanding the message. Lack of effective communication skills is a common blind spot for leaders because most of them believe that they are decent communicators. After all, how often do peers or direct reports raise their hands in a meeting to inform a leader he is communicating poorly? The absence of constructive criticism sometimes leads people to believe there is nothing to criticize.

So what causes the gap between perception and reality? The answer often lies in the audience. People interpret information in countless different ways, which is why there isn't just one right way to communicate. What makes perfect sense to some people may seem vague or confusing to others. In addition, the communication norms expected in some work cultures may seem inappropriate in others. That's why such an important part of communication is being able to gauge how the audience is interpreting the message, and to adjust it if necessary. One size does not fit all when it comes to communication. Remember, just because someone has been a good communicator in the past doesn't mean he is destined to always be a good communicator.

What a Poor Communicator Looks Like

Research shows that personality is a key determinant of people's ability or inability to behave in the workplace. Personality assessments capture aspects of personality that predict behavior. The Hogan Development Survey (HDS) assesses the dark side of personality, identifying toxic and nonproductive behaviors that can and do derail careers. The table that follows identifies the three HDS scales that a Poor Communicator will typically score high on (7 or greater on a 10-point scale). Poor Communicators are often unclear and will provide contradictory information. It is not unusual to find

The Poor Communicator's Leadershit Behaviors	
Three Highest *HDS Scores	How the Poor Communicator will behave in the workplace based on *HDS scores
Reserved	Interpersonally insensitive, prefers to work alone, uncomfortable around strangers, uncommunicative, feedback deficient, reserved, not a team player
Dutiful	Compliant, reluctant decision-maker, unwilling to challenge status quo, conforming, strong desire to please others, doesn't stand up for subordinates.
Cautious	Slow decision making, resistant to change, reluctant to take chances, motivated not to fail, unassertive, conservative, perceived as holding others back
Examples	Donald Sterling
*The Hogan Development Survey (HDS) evaluates the dark side of personality, identifying overused strengths and toxic assets that will derail careers if the behaviors are not kept in check.	

them struggling with a foot in their mouth. These leaders are perceived as reserved, reluctant to make decisions, and unwilling to challenge the status quo.

The Importance of Tailoring the Message to the Audience

Sally had worked in sales at a large organization for many years where she and her team consistently met their performance goals. Sally was thrilled when she was promoted to an executive sales position leading an even larger team. Her career was starting to take off, and people began noticing.

A few years later, Sally was presented with the opportunity to lead a professional organization whose members were successful executives. Sally saw this as a phenomenal opportunity, so she accepted the role of president, receiving strong support from the organization's board and influential members. Sally was on a roll, feeling confident with her leadership and communication skills.

Even though some members initially thought Sally was a bit over-the-top in terms of energy, few could argue that her first short speeches on the organization's vision weren't passionate and inspiring.

And then the first board and committee meetings took place. After the initial welcome events, people expected Sally to lead in an organized, straightforward way and have a clear plan for the future of the organization. What they got was the opposite. Sally was perceived as unclear, disorganized, and she changed her mind often. Her behavior and style combined with unusually high energy made her communication choppy, unclear, and volatile. What happened to sales executive Sally who everyone loved? In less than a year, the board was in chaos. Board members were feeling misdirected, frustrated, and exhausted— not to mention slightly bitter to be exerting so much energy outside of their day jobs. To make matters worse, the board members didn't feel comfortable giving Sally the feedback she needed about her leadership style. They simply weren't accustomed to having that conversation with a peer.

Finally Sally took the initiative to talk with a coach and analyze her breakdowns. She was surprised to learn all arrows pointed to her undeveloped communication skills. At first, Sally learned that there was often a discrepancy in the message she meant to send and the one her colleagues received. Her messages were often ambiguous, causing people to believe they heard different things. She was surprised, as she did not have this issue managing her sales team. What became apparent was that her direct reports on the sales team felt comfortable asking for clarification; it was part of their culture. This was not the board's culture; the board members didn't know each other well and were reluctant to ask questions that could delay progress or waste time. Instead, they let meetings end without gaining a full understanding of the plans and each assumed the other members understood.

Another reason Sally had trouble communicating clearly was that the board issues were not black and white like they were with her sales team. Her sales representatives completed task-based projects with clearly defined expectations and goals; nothing was left to interpretation. Leading the professional association was a totally different story. After so many years of communicating with a certain style, Sally wasn't aware that her style might not be as effective to a different audience. On the board, no one reported to her, and they had higher expectations regarding effective communication. She needed to make some adjustments.

What Can We Learn From This Story?

Even if your leadership style is passionate, expressive, analytical, pragmatic or driven, you shouldn't use that to justify a lack of clarity or brevity in your communication. No one likes to have their time wasted by a presenter rambling through disorganized or repetitive thoughts. Regardless of your leadership style, you should strive to be an effective communicator. Your leadership style will influence your communication, but that should never be done at the expense of effectiveness.

Overcoming Nerves

Sometimes shyness is the root cause of being a Poor Communicator. I know a woman who is warm, engaging, passionate, and has an inspiring life story, but her deep fear of public speaking hinders her ability to communicate effectively with an audience. In a casual setting or a small group she is completely comfortable, but she freezes up immediately when giving a formal presentation. She has an awkward demeanor and has trouble organizing her thoughts. Her warmth and passion disappear and she comes across as scattered-brained and uninspiring.

The truth is there are many people in the world who have this problem. Fear of public speaking ranks second after the fear of death; it brings on such anxiety that people are unable to deliver a simple message, much less communicate it well and inspire others. Leaders who suffer from this fear can take actions to overcome it or at least decrease their fear enough to feel a little more comfortable in front of audiences.

Tips for Overcoming Nerves:

- ☐ Take an improvisational acting class. It will give you practice thinking on your feet and speaking in front of an audience. It can also help you to stop taking yourself so seriously when all eyes are on you.

- ☐ Join a Toastmasters group to practice speaking in front of audiences and gain some personalized feedback.

- ☐ Practice presentations relentlessly to the point that you're comfortable with the material and feel prepared. This will allow you to relax a little more during presentations.

☐ Try taking yoga, Tai Chi, or meditation classes to learn how to inhibit the brain's fight or flight response by changing your breathing. Belle Halpern, founder and CEO of Inspiring Educators, recommends this as a way to calm nerves naturally and holistically.

☐ Look into the innovative treatment options that have become more popular in recent years for treating panic over public speaking such as sleep therapy or hypnosis. Even though these aren't guaranteed solutions some people swear they work.

Storytelling

Keynote speaker and business performance consultant Ryan Estis has built his business around delivering presentations that both teach and motivate his audiences. Estis speaks at more than 75 events per year, including corporate meetings for many of the world's best-known brands. One of his secrets to communicating effectively and inspiring people is simple: storytelling.

Like many professionals, Estis sometimes gets that feeling of nervous excitement before he goes on stage. That's why he starts every keynote with a personal story that relates to the presentation topic. Not only does this approach grab people's attention (and draws them in), it gives Estis more confidence.

"When we tell real stories of things that happened to us, we *own* those stories. No one can say they've heard it before or that we aren't telling it right," says Estis. "Stories make it easier to relax on stage and be authentic—vulnerable even. "

The great thing about stories is that they don't require memorization. People can recall what happened to them without much effort and tell the story like they would tell it to a friend. The next time you prepare to speak before a large group, consider Estis' advice and open with a story. In fact, try adding a couple more stories during your presentation as well. They can serve as check-in points to calm you down, speak from your heart, and reengage the audience, if necessary.

Be Confident, but not Overly Confident

When you overestimate how good you are at something or how easy it will be to do, you can put yourself in a bad situation. Meet John, a knowledgeable and experienced global leader who is one of the most innovative experts in his industry. John's boss asked him to present at the annual board retreat. John's business was doing really well so the chairman focused and worked more with the executives whose businesses were struggling. John, known for being fast on his feet, was fully convinced that he could wing the board presentation. He spent minimal time preparing his presentation and even less time preparing his delivery. His great business results went unnoticed because of the poor content and poor delivery; John gave the impression that he was unprepared and didn't have the full command of his business. He was scattered and his presentation lacked a logical flow. By the time he stepped out of the boardroom, John had lost credibility and the confidence of the board. He created additional and unnecessary work for his boss, who had to back him up by defending him as a much better business leader than communicator. Despite all of that it would take a long time for John to recover his image with the board. It takes time for people to forget an experience with a bad communicator.

What Can We Learn From This Story?

- [ ] Preparing your speech and/or presentation is just as important as having the business results to back it up. In fact, not being able to tell the story in a clear and compelling way can hurt the perception of the business and the leader's personal reputation and credibility. People might question how good a person can be at delivering the work if she cannot even articulate the work that she is delivering.

- [ ] Sometimes confidence can work against you. More often than not, people who feel comfortable in their own skin don't feel the need to prepare and rehearse. They will more often than not come across as disorganized. Preparing gives the presenter an opportunity to put himself in the audience's shoes and think about whether the experience will be engaging and clear or frustrating and fuzzy.

Show Your Passion

Sometimes leaders have trouble communicating because their delivery is so dry or uninspiring that they kill their audience with boredom. Some of these Poor Communicators are aware they aren't enthusiastic speakers, but they don't know how to fix it; it's not like they can just flip a switch.

Even though captivating audiences might be a long shot, at least as a short-term goal, most people can adapt their speaking style and improve their presence through hard work. I've coached many leaders who are actively trying to improve their speaking skills. The biggest success factor is being passionate, believing in what's being talked about and emoting that passion.

Max, my coaching client, found it difficult to show the enthusiasm he felt for his company, which made it difficult for others to see that he felt any passion. Max claimed that he was raised in a culture where emoting and demonstrating too much excitement in a business or social setting was considered inappropriate. I found this intriguing, because during our causal conversations, he would absolutely light up when he talked about his kids. He would get a twinkle in his eye and speak animatedly about soccer games and school projects, losing his inhibitions and speaking from the heart. These stories were interesting and I was genuinely drawn in and engaged. The minute we switched to talking business all of that was gone.

When I pointed out to Max this vast difference in communication style between how he discussed company business and how he discussed his children, he reaffirmed that he was always taught that business was a formal affair; professionalism was an important value and this meant it wasn't personal and definitely not emotional. As such, Max had approached his career in a professional manner, which came across as guarded, detached, and passionless. As a leader and frequent speaker, people found him uninspiring because they couldn't feel his passion for the company, its mission, and/or his role.

This coaching session was a turning point for Max. When he understood it was okay to use more of his personality and passion in the workplace, he opened up, relaxed, and had more meaningful conversations with his colleagues.

Tips for Showing Passion

☐ When something doesn't come naturally, practice can make a big difference. A great way to help people discover and emote their passion is to make them defend their viewpoints. For example, when coaching clients, I will use an exercise where I start speaking negatively about their companies and roles. Then I encourage them to argue with me. I'll say to someone, "So what if your company's products are helping people. What does it matter?" That opposition often sparks an emotional reaction where the individual's whole demeanor changes. I typically notice a variety of improvements in their communication style. The improvements correlate with being inspiring: direct eye contact, powerful body language, increased range of tone and facial expressions, and more confidence. I point out this difference and tell people how much more convincing they are by just changing the way they talk about something. Try this with a coworker or friend if one of you needs a little help sharing your passion.

☐ Think about the intentions of your message beyond simply informing others. Belle Halpern, Founder and CEO of Inspiring Educators and author of *Leadership Presence*, recommends focusing on passionate purposes:

- o To welcome
- o To excite
- o To challenge
- o To reassure
- o To shake up
- o To motivate
- o To create a sense of urgency
- o To offer hope

Using a couple of these purposes can help leaders or anyone put more passion in their message by focusing on how to make a better impact on their audience.

Picking the Right Medium

Tailoring your message to the audience includes picking the right communication medium. Luckily, leaders have more communication methods to choose from than ever before. Ryan Estis

126

stresses the importance of finding a medium that makes leaders feel comfortable and more likely to communicate openly and often. "It's inexcusable to run a company today and not communicate with your people on a consistent basis," he says. "There are so many mediums—pick one that works for you."

Estis makes it clear that some leaders may be more effective through virtual communication rather than through public speaking. He assures leaders that they don't need to stand on a stage every time they make an announcement. "Communicate consistently through *some* medium—email, social media, or a newsletter—and it builds trust," Estis advises. "People learn more about you, who you are, and how you make decisions."

For leaders like Sally in the case study, supplementing face-to-face communication with written communication is a smart way to ensure you're getting ideas across and appropriately tailoring your messages. In addition, people often feel more comfortable asking questions if they can ask through a virtual medium, rather than taking the floor in front of many colleagues.

Best Practices for Responding and Relating to the Poor Communicator

☐ The first step in helping Poor Communicators improve is to give feedback when the message needs to be clearer. It may seem obvious to listeners when directions are unclear, but it's safe to say the speaker thinks what he's saying makes sense. Letting him know there is an opportunity to improve clarity can make a huge difference.

☐ Support a feedback-driven culture where employees at all levels are open to giving and receiving feedback. This will enable upward coaching for leaders who need it.

☐ Provide clear alternative examples of how the same message could have been communicated more clearly. Also provide feedback on how clear communication impacts the recipients, the perception of the business, and ultimately, how it reflects on the presenter.

☐ If the poor communicator reports to you, invite him to present to you as if he was presenting to the board. You should have him practice as much as he needs to become comfortable.

☐ If you report to the Poor Communicator, you should offer to be a sounding board to him before big presentations. This way you are not just offering constructive criticism, but helping craft a solution.

Personalized Coaching

Sometimes it's best for Poor Communicators to work with an expert outside of the company; someone who can analyze their communication strengths and weaknesses and help them improve. Danny Slomoff, PhD, is a Communication Strategy expert who helps people communicate more effectively in the workplace. Slomoff and experts like him help demystify the communication process for professionals.

A few years ago, the CEO of a technology company approached Slomoff for coaching. He said, "I'm a good business executive and I've made money for my company. But I'm a poor communicator and I want to change that." The CEO sent Slomoff films from two recent presentations: it was clear the audience was disengaged. Half of the chairs were empty because people skipped the presentation. Those who showed up looked bored or confused. Slomoff could quickly see why—the presentation was full of complex financial jargon and overly detailed charts and graphs.

Slomoff met with the CEO to discuss these issues. The first step was to make sure future messages were tailored to the audience. This didn't mean the CEO couldn't talk about complex financial matters; it meant that such a presentation was better suited for the finance department. If he wanted to address the entire company, the content needed to be more general and easier to understand. In addition to addressing content, Slomoff coached the CEO advising him to use his facial expressions, body language, and voice to engage his audience. Finally, they focused on transforming nerves and anxiety into expression.

The two worked together for a few years and the CEO put in a lot of effort. He experienced vast improvements and became such a great speaker that he was invited to keynote global conferences. Even after his retirement, he continued giving an occasional keynote in his free time.

Experiencing this level of success in only a few years is unlikely without personalized coaching. Some executives pay for it out-of-pocket and others work it into the company's budget for all senior executives. Either way, it's often a worthwhile investment for Poor Communicators who have the drive to improve.

A Self-Improvement Plan

If you see a glimpse of the Poor Communicator in yourself, you certainly are not alone. We all have moments when we can't seem to find the right words to convey what we want to say. Luckily, it's easy to start making immediate improvements. You can learn and develop by doing and observing. Take action on the following tips to start incorporating more communication best practices into your day-to-day work life.

Giving Presentations

- Prepare, prepare, prepare: This includes creating presentation notes, choosing your words, timing your delivery, thinking about audience questions, and rehearsing many times. Watch yourself in front of the mirror while you speak. Even better, practice a dry run with a colleague or friend. If your boss knows your audience, she may be the best person to go through a dry run with you. After all, it is in her best interest that you are effective.

- Keep all of the important facts and information on hand even if you don't present this information, you may be asked. As a leader, you can't afford to be seen as unprepared.

- If you are not naturally funny, you should avoid making jokes that you think will be funny. Don't force the issue—the delivery is likely to come across as awkward, but not humorous.

- Don't make up fake case studies or stories to prove a point. People can sniff them out. There is a global products company who publically acknowledged unbelievable stories by using the code word interesting. It didn't take long for employees to realize what an interesting comment meant in the middle of a presentation.

- Be aware of how frequently you tell certain stories or give examples. Leaders who are enamored with their stories don't notice the eyes rolling or glazing over with boredom when they tell the same tale yet again.

- Avoid clichés, slogans, and buzzwords. Leaders who lean on these terms too often have no idea how much employees mock their communication. Have you ever heard of Buzzword Bingo (a.k.a. Bullshit

Bingo)? Employees play this game with overused business expressions as a means of mocking empty communication. It can sound something like this: "We plan on *touching base* with *out-of-the-loop stakeholders offline* to *restructure* the *granular* aspects of the *timeline...*" Using these terms might have your audience whooping for joy, but for all the wrong reasons. It is empty content, but sounds like something important. Business jargon is frequently overused to the point where it's funny or distracting and becomes ineffective.

One-on-One Conversations

Interacting with a smaller audience doesn't mean you shouldn't prepare effective communication. Often one-on-one communication is even more important than team communication. Because these conversations may have a more serious goal, making word choice, tone, and delivery are even more important. Leaders may be Ineffective with one on-one communication for a variety of reasons. Perhaps, they are conflict-averse, unprepared, or cannot balance talking and listening to create good two-way dialog. It is important to evaluate and identify changes that could improve your one-on-one communication skills.

Before each important one-on-one interaction, ask yourself:

☐ What outcomes do I want from this discussion, and what specific requests do I have?

☐ What does the other party want to get out of this discussion and what specific requests might they have?

☐ What are the known facts regarding the particular subject that will be discussed?

☐ What environmental and emotional contexts surround this discussion?

Conduct this brief exercise to prepare before important one-on-one conversations and compare the results with past conversations where you were not prepared. If you still struggle to understand opportunities for improvement, you should seek feedback from someone you trust who will give you their unvarnished opinion.

Even though many of these tips seem to be common sense, many people are so confident in their communication and presentation skills that they don't take the time to do any of these things. Good communication can come more naturally to some people than it does to others; however, the best communicators invest a lot of time preparing their communication and honing their skills.

Summary

Your effectiveness as a communicator—both with one-on-one and larger audiences—definitely shapes the perception others have of you as a leader. It is worth the time and effort to improve your communication skills so that you can put your best foot forward. In fact, good communication may be the difference between being passed up or moving up in an organization. My best advice: work on your communication skills so that the former doesn't happen to you, but the latter does.

CHAPTER ELEVEN

THE BAD FIRST IMPRESSIONIST

Starting a new job is an exciting time, but it is easy to forget how hard it can be. It might be especially difficult for experienced leaders who might be out of practice when it comes to learning a new position. New hires are expected to become familiar with their new roles, the company, responsibilities, boss, and coworkers; in addition, new leaders have to guide a new team. At first, the new direct reports may be like watchdogs, analyzing the new manager's every move and trying to determine what's in store for them under new leadership. This can create a tricky situation even for seasoned leaders who want to do a good job, but also want to be liked by everyone—their boss, the board of directors, peers, and direct reports. In those first few days and weeks at a new organization, the pressure to do well and gain acceptance can cause new-hires to act in ways that do more harm than good. Because new leaders, especially those coming from the outside, aren't likely to have a deep understanding of the culture, it's difficult for them to anticipate how others might perceive their words and actions. Unfortunately, insider knowledge of the culture isn't typically part of a company's formal onboarding program; this leaves new-hires to read between the lines and figure it out themselves.

Having coached many senior executives through the onboarding process, I have my share of horror stories. When a leader's integration with a new company isn't going well, it's typically the result of behavioral or communication mistakes. The new-hire may be doing something that rubs people the wrong way, but he or she is oblivious to it. There are a handful of behaviors that tend to be the source of new-hires' problems, but the new hire often doesn't understand that these behaviors are not being well-received by colleagues. These blind spots become especially problematic for new employees because they haven't earned the benefit of the doubt from colleagues.

What Bad First Impressionists Look Like

Research shows that personality is a key determinant of people's ability or inability to behave in the workplace. Personality assessments capture aspects of personality that predict behavior. The Hogan Development Survey (HDS) assesses the dark side of personality, identifying toxic and

The Bad First Impressionist's Leadershit Behaviors	
Three Highest *HDS Scores	How the Bad First Impressionist will behave in the workplace based on *HDS scores
Colorful	Self-promoting, attention seeking, poor listening skills, easily distracted, manages by crisis, problems with organization, lacks follow-though
Imaginative	Different perspectives and ideas, poor influence and persuasions skills, whimsical and eccentric, potentially creative but off the mark, preoccupied, unconventional unaware of how their actions affect others.
Bold	Resistant to feedback, overestimates talents and accomplishments, doesn't seek different opinions, demanding and overbearing, blames mistakes on others, self-promoting, strong sense of entitlement, no team loyalty
Examples	Howard Cosell, Donald Trump
*The Hogan Development Survey (HDS) evaluates the dark side of personality, identifying overused strengths and toxic assets that will derail careers if the behaviors are not kept in check.	

nonproductive behaviors that can and do derail careers. The table that follows identifies the three HDS scales that the Bad First Impressionist will typically score high on (7 or greater on a 10-point scale). These individuals are often anxious to please and sometimes appear arrogant. Often these leaders are trying very hard to be accepted, but they are perceived as outspoken, self-promoting, poor listeners, and maybe even as show-offs.

This chapter highlights the top mistakes a leader, manager or an individual contributor can make when starting in a new role and explains how to avoid these mistakes. We will also offer tips on how to respond to onboarding leadershit when you are the lucky recipient of a clueless new boss or colleague.

Mistake #1 – Being a Show-off

Everyone wants to be seen as competent in a new role, but sometimes new-hires focus so much on proving themselves that they can come across as arrogant and unlikeable. John, the head of an insurance practice for a premier consulting firm, learned this the hard way when he left his longtime job for one at an insurance company. John was accustomed to the culture at his former company where a high premium was placed on employees demonstrating that they were the smartest person in the room. People spent more time in meetings thinking about the most insightful comment they could make rather than really listening to what other people said. And God forbid that someone made an especially clever comment, because then everyone's focus would be on how to make an even smarter comment. John was immersed in this culture for so long that it became his normal method of operating. Unfortunately, norms were quite different at his new organization: people proved themselves through success in the marketplace and typically avoided speaking about their own accomplishments. As you can see, this clash of workplace cultures was a disaster waiting to happen for John.

When John was invited to his first company meetings, he prepared by focusing on how he could appear smart, aggressive, knowledgeable and, of course, more valuable than his peers. After all, that was the behavior that made people excel at his former company. During the meetings, John dove right in. He did more talking than listening and asserted his intellectual superiority at every opportunity. He lacked self-awareness; he didn't see that he was creating a reputation as an arrogant and domineering leader.

When a leader starts building a bad reputation early on, it's unlikely anyone will tell him. That level of openness and trust has not yet been built.

Not only did John damage his likability, but also he missed out on a unique opportunity to learn about the business, employees, and clients from key stakeholders. Being new presented John the perfect chance to build relationships and trust. In return, employees might have informally provided him with company information that might not have been available in company documents. However, because John alienated his colleagues right from the start, they never bothered to share insider information with him. In fact, because others perceived him as a self-serving political beast, they started to keep their valuable insights and information to themselves so they could look smart and valuable in meetings. Just think about the kind of new and toxic dynamics John was inadvertently introducing into the workplace. And because John talked most of the time, he missed the chance to understand people's real agendas and motivations.

A Better Approach

☐ Listen: First-time interactions with new coworkers are a great time to focus on listening instead of talking. This allows you to learn about the company culture, which will help you to communicate more effectively. New-hires can and certainly should share their opinions, but doing so should be secondary to listening during onboarding.

- ☐ Stop Selling: For new hires there is often a thin line between demonstrating wisdom and experience and being arrogant and annoying. Once people cross that line and are perceived as arrogant, coworkers have a more difficult time listening with an open mind and accepting them. After you start your new job, remember to snap out of the interview mode. Stop selling yourself and begin delivering on your promises. Starting off on the wrong foot will close more doors than it opens.

- ☐ Focus on Learning: You can only be the new kid for a short time. However, that timeframe can be quite beneficial when played well. During this short window, learn as much as you can. Ask questions; listen to the responses. Use this time wisely and focus on learning.

Mistake #2 – Ready, Fire, Aim: There's a New Sheriff in Town

Replacing a leader comes with its own set of challenges whether the past leader was well liked or not. Some new leaders think it's best to show their authority by making changes immediately. Even though some quick changes can be smart, many leaders get trigger-happy and employ the ready-fire-aim method. They update policies or change decisions before they learn enough to fully assess the situation and understand the implications of their actions.

Much of the day-to-day work activity hinges on a leader's goals and personal preferences. When small things change here or there, a lot of people can be affected. The goal is to lead the type of change that people can feel positive about. Often, this is easier said than done.

I recently had lunch with a friend who works in human resources for a global manufacturing company. Their Chief Information Officer (CIO) had resigned a few months earlier and a woman named Alex had been selected for the open position. My friend told me Alex knew she had a tough act to follow. The long-tenured former CIO was adored by his employees and had successfully led a global enterprise system implementation; he was surely going to be missed. To make the transition even more difficult, Alex knew the CEO and the board had considered two external and two internal candidates before selecting Alex, one of the external candidates. Needless to say the internal candidates were quite disappointed about not getting the big job.

Alex anticipated that her new colleagues and direct reports would be apprehensive and possibly resistant to changes. Alex thought this made it even more important to set the tone for change as early as possible to establish herself as the new CIO. In the first days and weeks, Alex started making major changes to department policies and procedures and turned a smooth-running machine into a bunch of parts that could no longer function together.

The key problem with Alex's approach was that as an outsider, she wasn't aware of unintended consequences that her changes could create. Furthermore, immediately dismantling what the previous beloved CIO had put in place without a sound business rationale was particularly unpopular. Not only was the staff upset about the chaos that resulted from unwise changes, they were now scared about the organization's (and their) futures.

Alex had a limited amount of time to establish herself and demonstrate that she was a strong leader even though she was different from the previous CIO. Unfortunately, she did it all wrong.

A Better Approach

A better approach for a new leader in a similar situation would be to focus on subtle, but visible, harmless changes instead of radical ones. Why? Because in your first few weeks no matter how talented you are, you simply don't know enough to make drastic changes. You don't know the implications, unintended or undesired consequences of such changes. However, you don't need a deep understanding of the company to make minor changes that send a message about how you will lead differently than your predecessor.

For example, several years ago I took the place of a long tenured colleague in a professional services organization. Historically he held business development calls that included only senior partners and he controlled the agenda. When I started, my first changes were to add junior partners to the meetings and I circulated a request for agenda topics. I also changed the weekly meeting schedule from Mondays to Fridays. These minor changes were meant to send a clear message about who was in charge; it also hinted at the type of culture I intended to foster—one that was inclusive and participative.

In another instance, I worked with a new CEO who replaced a strong and conservative leader. The company was in the midst of a major turnaround so many changes were in the works; the new CEO needed buy-in at all levels. During the first couple of days in his new role, he started having lunch in the employee cafeteria, which was something the old CEO never did. He also changed the company dress code from business casual to casual, allowing employees to wear jeans. These actions sent a message that there was a new and different type of leader in charge and showed the type of culture employees could expect to see in the future.

When making initial changes in a new role, you might focus on showing employees that you are different than your predecessor—not that you think you are better.

Mistake #3 – Taking the Fifth on Vision and Strategy

The opposite of the Ready-Fire-Aim Sheriff is taking the Fifth, which is lack of guidance and direction. Instead of being trigger-happy and implementing radical changes, this new-hire doesn't shoot, rather he keeps his vision and plan to himself, leaving colleagues and direct reports uninformed and confused.

Ted, a thoughtful and reserved new leader, had always been a slow decision maker. When he took over a private company in the Midwest, he decided he would listen and observe before making changes. Ted spent a lot of time taking it all in, but not sharing any of his observations, ideas, or thoughts with his staff. What Ted didn't know was that employees wanted to hear from him and understand his plans; they needed to know how much change to expect. In the absence of communication, employees started to speculate and make assumptions. Were they being excluded from the strategic plan because they were all going to be fired? Was the company downsizing and outsourcing responsibilities? The staff braced themselves for what they thought was on the horizon. The culture quickly became fear-based and the long-standing trust in senior leadership was gone. When Ted was ready to communicate his plan and implement changes, employees trusted him less than when he first started working with them. This lack of informing them had damaged his credibility.

A Better Approach

From the moment you set foot in your new office, colleagues will be curious about your plan for moving the organization forward. In the absence of clear discussions and reassurance, employees tend to create stories to fill in the communication gaps. They don't do it because they like gossip, are vicious, or want the new leader to fail; they do it because they are human beings who are motivated by clear information and direction.

Regardless of your business vision and strategy, it's in your best interest to communicate this to your direct reports and colleagues. If you choose not to be forthcoming with information, you will spend even more time addressing rumors and gossip, and conducting damage control. Great leadership is all about clear communication, guidance, and being courageous enough to make and share decisions with others. So, don't shy away from making important decisions and sharing your strategy with those around you.

Mistake #4 – The Secret Agent

When stepping into a new leadership role, it's easy to make assumptions. You assume colleagues know the organizational hierarchy and understand the basic expectations of different positions and departments. However, when a new role is created, employees are often left in the dark. Sometimes their boss fails to communicate the duties and authority of this new role to the rest of the company. This oversight can cause serious problems for a new leader as well as existing team members.

A few years ago, Mary took a new job at a global manufacturing company headquartered in Japan. An experienced executive, she was told that in her new role she was to be a change agent and transform the Japanese-centric culture into a more global one. However, the senior leaders who hired her never informed employees that cultural transformation was a companywide goal and that Mary was hired to aggressively lead this initiative.

As soon as our enthusiastic and eager-to-deliver secret change agent tried to lead cultural change, it caused confusion and surprise. Ultimately, resistance surfaced in the ranks, especially among Mary's peers. Whenever Mary offered ideas about change, her colleagues exchanged looks as if she had landed from another planet. Mary's peers asked each other questions like, "Who does she think she is?" or, "Is she serious?" Mary was quickly seen as arrogant, insensitive, and overpowering. Her coworkers were uncooperative, making Mary's job even harder. Mary grew more and more frustrated with her inability to get things done. As her frustration grew, so did her rough edges. Her employees saw the writing on the wall for their newly minted boss and made sure not to get too close to her. Any hope of garnering the support and resources to accomplish what she was brought in to do had vanished within the first couple of weeks and never returned. Mary's focus on culture change combined with the disconnect between her charter and what the organization perceived it to be created a disastrous situation. Within a year Mary was gone.

Mary, who assumed everybody was on the same page regarding her role, demonstrated leadershit. Her boss also added to the situation because he failed to communicate the responsibilities for her role throughout the company. Remember that it is important to make transparency a priority in the onboarding process.

A Better Approach

- [ ] Don't assume: When stepping into a new role, never assume that colleagues, peers, and direct reports are clear on the new role's responsibilities. Make sure others have the same understanding that is articulated by your boss or other leadership. More often than not, employees don't know what you were hired to do. This oversight can cause serious problems for any new-hire, especially for a new leader. Make it your responsibility to initiate a conversation that ensures everyone is on the same page.

- [ ] Speak up: If you are reporting to a Mary in your organization, you may see the problem more clearly than your new boss. If there is a gap between what Mary says she's been hired to do and how other departments view her role, speak up. Mary needs supporters to help her navigate the situation.

Helping Mary see the disconnect between her vision and others' visions of her role can positively change her onboarding; this is something she won't soon forget. Quite frankly, Mary's gratitude could dramatically improve the quality of your professional life as well.

A Plan to be a Better Leader

Every time you start a new job even within the same company, you should see the role as a unique opportunity to reinvent yourself; it is a time to rethink who you want to be as a leader and maybe even change the trajectory of your career. The assumption that you know it all or that what made you successful in the past will make you successful in the future is an arrogant and limited way to embrace your new role.

Reputation Management

Reputation and image are often a new-hire's greatest concerns. Rightfully so, because so much of professional success depends on what people think of you. If you developed a negative reputation in your last position, it's important to be aware that it might follow you. With today's social media outlets, gossip can spread like wildfire and your bad reputation can easily precede you. Employees are naturally curious about their new boss and are especially adept at seeking and discovering this kind of information.

Regardless of your reputation at your last job, your new coworkers will have a perception of you before your first day. Whether a senior leader or human resources director provided a high-level overview of your background or team members have looked you up on LinkedIn, people will have formed opinions about you. During the first few days in your new role, you can choose to ignore their preconceived notions, or you can invite yourself into the discussion about who you are and what you are all about. This allows you to be proactive about disclosing what people are actually interested in or what you want them to know about you, such as:

- ☐ Your strengths

- ☐ Your experiences

- ☐ What you are working on from a personal development perspective

- ☐ What is negotiable and non-negotiable for you

- ☐ What people can expect from you

- ☐ What you expect from them

You can initiate this type of conversation easily as a new-hire in one-on-one meetings or in a group setting. Many people choose to make it a casual exchange, but it can be done in a formal presentation as well. The medium is not as important as the message.

One of the most courageous examples of self-disclosure I have seen from a new employee was provided by my friend David, who took a position as a high level executive in a global manufacturing company headquartered in Asia. David is American, but had spent his entire career working for European companies. His background added diversity, but he realized this could also make seeing eye-to-eye with colleagues a greater challenge.

A few weeks into the job, the leadership team had a multi-day strategy meeting; one day was dedicated to getting to know each other. Each employee, new and long-tenured, was asked to share his or her work experience and background. David, in addition to discussing the basics, created a slide deck and candidly shared his values, strengths, and developmental areas; this included both good and bad headlines from previous 360 evaluations. At the end of his presentation, he gave his new team explicit permission to give him feedback every time he was doing something that violated the key principles or values they discussed. He shared his expectations of the team, what they could expect from him and his list of non-negotiable items. This might seem like a risky strategy, but at the end of the day, Dave had earned a high level of respect and built a reputation of authenticity. He could only destroy it if he didn't live up to the values, principles, and beliefs he had proudly promised.

A Strategic Communication Plan

When you join a new organization, work with your boss, a human resources leader, or a mentor to create a list of individuals you should meet with during your first week, month, and quarter. This list should include: key employees, peers, managers, customers, external partners, suppliers, human resources employees, and others from key functions. These meetings will help you learn how stakeholders think and feel about the business and the people involved. This stakeholder management plan is equivalent to a business plan, except with a laser focus on people. Use these first meetings to ask questions about:

1. The views and expectations people have about your role or unit;

2. The culture of the organization as they see it; and,

3. How decisions are made and how things get done.

   ☐ Focus on listening, learning, and empathizing with stakeholders. If people are open, you can learn what is working and what needs to be evaluated or changed.

- Don't take all opinions at face value. Take copious notes in every meeting, save them, and review them six months later. You will be surprised by how much more deeply you understand the meaning of what people were telling you at the outset.

- Finally, use these first meetings to create a people-map. Identify influencers, connectors, blockers, givers, and takers. This will help you understand whom you should relate to, whom you should watch or avoid, and whom you should partner with to create results.

In addition to scheduling these meetings, ask early about the company's operating and management routines. What regular meetings, calls, functions, and webinars are you expected to attend? Inquire about mandatory commitments versus optional ones. After all, you won't want to miss the monthly TGIF meeting where key business connections really happen

Summary

Starting in a new professional role is exciting, bringing with it powerful lessons in culture and diversity. Each individual's personality, work, and leadership styles are different. These styles and behaviors combine to form an organization's social norms and cultural identity. Starting a new job can feel like connecting with old friends or landing on another planet; we might not know which situation we're going to get into until we are on board. In these times of uncertainty, the smartest option is to be prepared. New-hires should take responsibility for successfully onboarding by avoiding the worst practices described in this chapter. As you have read, everywhere you turn you can make mistakes or take a misstep. Even if you have a plan, not everything will go as planned. However, maintaining a high level of personal awareness and having a thoughtful strategy can make a huge difference.

Onboarding is a great learning experience, but only for those who choose to pay attention. If you aren't currently in a new role, watch the new-hires and observe what's going well for them and what isn't. Take notes on the behaviors you would like to emulate and the pitfalls you want to avoid. If your organization could be better supporting new-hires, let executives or human resources know. When you help others onboard, you will be helping yourself prepare for future success.

CHAPTER TWELVE

LEADERSHIT TRANSFORMATION

This book highlights the negative behaviors in the workplace, because these are the situations that most people experience, and the ones in which people need the most help. There are thousands of books available that highlight best practices and positive leadership examples in the workplace, but all too often, those examples look nothing like the daily work environment. In most professional environments, things are far from perfect. I don't mean this to be a depressing fact—it is just reality. Being a manager or leader is difficult and most people do the best they can at any given moment. Perfection in the workplace is an unreasonable expectation, but in all organizations there is room for improvement.

> **The best person to drive change is you; the best way to drive change is to lead it; the best way to lead it is to model the behaviors you want to see.**

The best person to drive change is you; the best way to drive change is to lead it; the best way to lead it is to model the behaviors you want to see. Do some personal reflection and think hard about these leadershit profiles. Do you see any of these tendencies in your behavior? Try to see yourself through your coworkers' eyes. At times, have you been unaccountable or deliberately avoided being transparent with your team, even if you had good reasons? Do you tend to agree with your boss no matter what she says? Or have you been using more than your fair share of company resources?

If any of these actions rings a bell, you have some work to do. First and foremost, don't beat yourself up about it. Even though many of the leadershit behaviors we discuss in this book are the most extreme examples and stereotypes, it's important to note that no leader is perfect. Even the best leaders have moments where they exhibit some type of leadershit behavior, whether it's communicating poorly, losing their temper, or putting their foot in their mouth. The true problem isn't creating isolated unpleasant incidents; it is when people become one of the profiles in this book. That means the offensive behavior has escalated in frequency and intensity; now the leader spends a noticeable amount of time in leadershit mode. It's important to dig deep and be honest with yourself. Do you rarely exhibit leadershit tendencies or have you become one of the profiles? Either way you have an opportunity for leadershit transformation.

The following **Leadership Imperatives** will help you transform leader*shit* into true leader*ship*:

1) **Self-awareness**

   The first step toward leadershit transformation is recognizing the problem. We tend to describe ourselves as who we would like to be rather than who we are or how others experience us. Some people are naturally capable of looking at themselves in the mirror and spotting all of their pimples. A far greater number of people are incapable of seeing areas for improvement, and/or recognizing situations that will derail their best intentions. These individuals often need other people to give them feedback on how they are behaving and how their behavior affects others. Self-awareness is like a muscle that shrinks when not used and gets stronger when exercised. So don't be afraid to exercise your self-awareness muscle.

When you become self-aware, you become acutely sensitive to the impact you have on others. You are more thoughtful about how you make decisions, how you respond to circumstances, and how you get results. This awareness level contributes to becoming a great leader.

2) **Authentic Change**

After you become aware of your improvement areas, you have to decide if you care enough to take action and make real change. Many leaders who fit these leadershit profiles know they are behaving badly. They know they are manipulative, or noncommittal, or downright mean; yet, they don't care enough to change. It takes hard work to become a better version of yourself, and people aren't always willing to make the effort.

Some leaders are willing to change temporarily because they see it as a means to achieve something they want. For example, if their boss asks them to become less rough around the edges, they will dial their bad behavior back until they get their promotion or reward. After they proved themselves and/or get their promotion, they will often go right back to their old ways especially if the change was extrinsically motivated.

To foster authentic change, people must be intrinsically motivated to improve; they must want to become better for personal reasons rather than the next promotion or pay increase. Reasons that come from inside don't often have an elaborate explanation.

3) **Adaptability**

Changing your ways means questioning your deeply rooted paradigms and beliefs. That requires a great deal of flexibility and adaptability. Again, some people are wired to be flexible and can adapt easily, but others need to learn how to develop that capability. It's possible to become more adaptable, but it requires clear intention, commitment, and hard work.

4) **Courage and resilience**

Doing the right thing isn't always easy. As we mentioned in previous chapters, doing the right thing may require taking unpopular stands or not always siding with your boss on issues. That's why transforming from leadershit to leadership takes courage. You need to persevere through challenging conditions even when others give up. Great leaders exhibit courage and resilience.

5) **Empathy**

Great leaders are able to put themselves in other people's shoes, whether they are making tough calls or having the difficult conversations. They stick with the decisions they believe are the right ones, but acknowledge the impact of those decisions on certain situations or individuals. If there is a negative impact or collateral damage to stakeholders, great leaders exhibit empathy rather than skirting responsibility. They also explain why a certain decision was made and why it was the right course of action. Finally, they acknowledge and take responsibility for any negative impact that the decision may have created. This behavior garners understanding, respect, and empathy from the leader.

6) **Humble confidence**

You should decisively lead the way, but constantly reflect on whether there is a better way to get to results. In order to do that, you need to be humble enough to listen and be open to learning from others. Humble confidence implies being attentive to every piece of information, all data available. It means moving forward while sensing every movement in your surroundings. Leaders exhibit humble confidence by being comfortable in their own skin and responding sincerely through their actions and reactions.

7) **Relentless and creative optimism**

Great leaders don't give up easily. They persevere in the face of adversity and stand for what they believe in. When they hit a brick wall, they make creative adjustments to achieve the desired results in a different way. They have a can-do attitude that is fueled by creative thinking. This behavior is often so contagious that it boosts new energy even in those who were about to declare defeat.

8) **Doing the right thing**

Great leaders have an amazing capacity to cut through the noise and focus on doing the right thing. They do this independent of their personal goals, agendas, or values. They are true team players and put other people and the company before their personal interests.

These leadership attributes are critical to successfully transform from leadershit to leadership. When you **see** these behavioral standards in action, it's clear that you have a real leader in your midst.

Taking a Stand Against Leadershit

Focusing on self-improvement can only go so far. Just as you aren't perfect, neither are your peers, your direct reports, or your boss. In fact, after learning about the types of leadershit in the workplace, you've probably thought about certain coworkers, both past and present. No doubt various things people said or did always rubbed you the wrong way and now you understand why—pure and simple leadershit.

It is my hope that this simple affirmation will give you the courage required to take a stand against unacceptable behavior in the workplace. Leadershit causes stress and so many other issues for both individuals and companies. Please don't turn a blind eye to it. Ignoring the problem will not make it go away or make it better. Quite the opposite. Left unchecked and unchallenged, bad leaders typically gain more power and become more brutal. Furthermore, they usually break down the people around them.

As professionals, we need to raise our standards for what is considered acceptable workplace behavior.

We may find ourselves responding to bad behavior in ways that don't make us proud; that's because bad leaders know how to bring out the worst in us. When we put up with leadershit for long periods, we become a lesser version of ourselves. For example, Tyrants or Users and Abusers belittle us, which can make us feel small and insignificant; we internalize that feeling and it can affect who we are at the core. The result is like an abusive relationship. No one deserves to be treated that way.

Top Ways to Take a Stand

Document: When you start to notice leadershit behaviors, document all interactions with that person. Whenever possible, speak to that person in groups rather than one-on-one. Send follow-up emails that summarize the conversations. Collect data that establishes a clear-cut case for what that person said versus what he or she actually did.

Have a direct conversation: If the leadershit offender is a direct report, it is your responsibility to have a candid conversation about acceptable behavior. If the person is a peer, you should tactfully and unemotionally bring up your concerns. Use documented proof if you have it. If the person is your boss, it is a more difficult situation. If your boss is open to feedback, you can try a direct approach. If not, it may work better to speak with human resources about your issues. Again, using documented proof of poor behavior can make a huge difference in supporting your case.

Share feedback in 360 reviews or the employee survey: If It doesn't seem smart to have a direct conversation, provide honest feedback when it is solicited through 360 reviews or employee surveys. Senior leaders do review this feedback and it helps them plan for the future. It could take time to see real change, but it can certainly get the ball rolling.

If nothing else works, find a better company and job: There comes a point when you should ask yourself if it's worth it to stay in a toxic environment. You may have put in years of hard work, persevered through unfair situations, and have planned to stick it out until things got better. But the reality is that your situation might not improve, or it may take years to do so. Ask yourself if it's worth it to stay. If the answer is no, maybe you should look around and see what companies are hiring.

Great employees deserve better than to experience leadershit day in and day out. Whether you're at the bottom of the organizational hierarchy or the top, you deserve a positive and productive working environment. As professionals, we need to raise our standards for what is considered acceptable workplace behavior. To drive change, you may have to put yourself out there and take a risk, but it'll be worth it. Above all else, keep the faith that people can and will change. Although we are creatures of habit, human beings are incredibly adaptable and we can learn to improve. It takes some people longer than others, but life is a constant cycle of learning and evolving. No one is perfect, so the best we can do is to stay focused on improvement. If more people set out to do this in the workplace, I am confident we can transform leadershit into true leadership.

ABOUT THE AUTHOR

Ana Dutra, CEO of The Executives' Club, has over 28 years of business management, strategic growth, and executive consulting experience in 30-plus countries. Dutra helps Boards, CEOs and their teams with growth strategies, innovation, acquisitions, culture change, turnarounds and technology issues.

Ana worked globally for IBM and has served as CEO for Mandala Global Advisors and Korn/Ferry Consulting, where she completed and integrated acquisitions of several global product and services companies. She serves on boards for CME Group (CME-NASDAQ), Greeley and Hansen, Lurie Children's Hospital of Chicago, Academy for Urban School Leadership and the Committee of 200, among others.

Dutra frequently speaks at the Global Competitiveness and Economic Forum. She contributes to the online Harvard Business Review, Forbes, Wall Street Journal, CEO Magazine and was a guest editor of the 2015 Best of the Boardroom issue of Hispanic Executive magazine. Ana received the Chicago United Business Leader of Color and the Verizon Nueva Estrella Latina awards.

A native Brazilian, Ana holds an MBA from Kellogg, a Masters in Economics from Pontificia Universidade do Rio de Janeiro, a Juris Doctor from Universidade do Rio de Janeiro. She is an avid triathlete and yoga practitioner and the proud mother of three daughters.

Stay connected with Ana at www.LessonsinLeadershiT.com/

Made in the USA
Lexington, KY
23 October 2017